Being Red

A Politics for the Future

Ken Livingstone

Edited by Anna Minton,
on behalf of the Left Book Club

PlutoPress
www.plutobooks.com

First published 2016 by Pluto Press
345 Archway Road, London N6 5AA

www.plutobooks.com

Copyright © Ken Livingstone 2016
Chapter 6 copyright © Jan Woolf

The right of Ken Livingstone to be identified as the author of this work has
been asserted by him in accordance with the Copyright, Designs and Patents
Act 1988.

The Left Book Club, founded in 2014, company number 9338285, pays
homage to the original Left Book Club founded by Victor Gollancz in 1936.

Every effort has been made to trace copyright holders and to obtain their
permission for the use of copyright material in this book. The publisher
apologises for any errors or omissions in this respect and would be grateful if
notified of any corrections that should be incorporated in future reprints or
editions.

British Library Cataloguing in Publication Data
A catalogue record for this book is available from the British Library

ISBN   978 0 7453 9905 8   Paperback
ISBN   978 1 7837 1812 2   PDF eBook
ISBN   978 1 7837 1814 6   Kindle eBook
ISBN   978 1 7837 1813 9   EPUB eBook

This book is printed on paper suitable for recycling and made from fully
managed and sustained forest sources. Logging, pulping and manufacturing
processes are expected to conform to the environmental standards of the
country of origin.

Typeset by Stanford DTP Services, Northampton, England

Simultaneously printed in the European Union and United States of America

Being Red

Contents

List of Illustrations

Series Preface

The first Left Book Club (1936–48) had 57,000 members, had distributed 2 million books, and had formed 1,200 workplace and local groups by the time it peaked in 1939. LBC members were active throughout the labour and radical movement at the time, and the Club became an educational mass movement, remodelling British public opinion and contributing substantially to the Labour landslide of 1945 and the construction of the welfare state.

Publisher Victor Gollancz, the driving force, saw the LBC as a movement against poverty, fascism and the growing threat of war. He aimed to resist the tide of austerity and appeasement, and to present radical ideas for progressive social change in the interests of working people. The Club was about enlightenment, empowerment and collective organisation.

The world today faces a crisis on the scale of the 1930s. Capitalism is trapped in a long-term crisis. Financialisation and austerity are shrinking demand, deepening the depression and widening social inequalities. The social fabric is being torn apart. International relations are increasingly tense and militarised. War threatens on several fronts, while fascist and racist organisations are gaining ground across much of Europe. Global warming threatens the planet and the whole of humanity with climate catastrophe. Workplace organisation has been weakened, and social democratic parties have been hollowed out by acceptance of pro-market dogma. Society has become more atomised, and mainstream politics suffers an acute democratic deficit.

Yet the last decade has seen historically unprecedented levels of participation in street protest, implying a mass audience for radical alternatives. But socialist ideas are no longer, as in the immediate post-war period, 'in the tea'. One of neoliberalism's achievements has been to undermine ideas of solidarity, collective provision and public service.

The Left Book Club aspires to meet the ideological challenge posed by the global crisis. Our aim is to offer high-quality books at affordable prices that are carefully selected to address the central issues of the day and to be accessible to a wide general audience. Our list represents the full range of progressive traditions, perspectives and ideas. We hope the books will be used as the basis of reading circles, discussion groups, and other educational and cultural activities relevant to developing, sharing and disseminating ideas for radical change in the interests of the common people at home and abroad.

The Left Book Club collective

Editor's Preface

This book comes out at a time of tumultuous change and activity for the left in Britain, representing arguably the greatest upheaval in Labour politics since the schisms of the early 1980s. So it feels apt for the newly revived Left Book Club to bring out a book which spans the career of one of the left's most successful political figures. Until recently he appeared to have exited the stage, swapping politics for life with a young family, but with the election of Jeremy Corbyn as Labour leader he is firmly back in the public eye.

The genesis of the book came last year, when Ken approached the soon to relaunch Left Book Club with a view to publishing writing he had been working on about his relationship with Boris Johnson and his reflections on the future of the left in Britain.

Ken has already written a very comprehensive autobiography, *You Can't Say That*, and we felt that alongside his new writing, rather than reprising key episodes from his career, we wanted to take a more journalistic approach, highlighting central aspects that seem particularly relevant in today's political context. As a result we suggested to Ken that we intersperse his writing with a series of candid interviews addressing the wide range of issues and controversies he has been involved with, in a style in keeping with the Left Book Club's aim to provide compelling, accessible writing for a wide-ranging, politically engaged readership.

The result is three extensive interviews which complement Ken's own writing. The first interview covers his time as leader of the Greater London Council, which with the benefit of hindsight reflects that rarely achieved moment in politics when a politician breaks the mould and captures the changing spirit of the times. That contrasts with the more executive role of Mayor of London, which Ken held first as an independent after Tony Blair barred him from standing as the Labour candidate, and then later as a Labour Mayor, after he was readmitted to the Labour Party. In addition to these two pieces we wanted a far more personal interview that would provide a snapshot of his background, character and family relationships, which was carried out by the writer Angharad Penrhyn Jones, editor of the award-winning anthology *Here We Stand*.

One aspect of Ken's career that has often been overlooked is his support for artists and in particular his association with Peter Kennard, who was regarded as almost an artist-in-residence at the GLC. Writer Jan Woolf's essay, 'I Don't Know Much About Art But ...', offers a window into the relationship that Ken has maintained with the visual arts.

As the book started to take shape the political context changed dramatically with the election of Jeremy Corbyn as Labour leader. As commentators proclaimed that Corbyn was an old Labour dinosaur, the project became fascinating to me as I prepared for my interviews with Ken and researched the struggles on the left which had formed the backdrop to my childhood but were vague in outline and detail. For anyone over 50 with an interest in politics, the titanic struggles around the direction of the left and the controversies over caucuses and rate capping will be familiar. For anyone under 45 they become far more vague, while those under 40 often know next to nothing about them at all. This generation gap became abundantly clear as New Labour veterans of a certain age were unable to grasp how the support for Corbyn had swelled, while their dire warnings of a return to a politics of more than 30 years ago fell on deaf ears; these were old battles of little relevance for the predominantly young audience enthused by Corbyn.

Of equal interest to me was hearing Ken describe how New Labour had taken on the more undemocratic elements of old Labour's political tactics and used them against him to prevent him standing as Mayor of London. But just as Mrs Thatcher's abolition of the GLC and blatant disregard for democracy turned Ken into a popular hero for Londoners, Tony Blair had the same impact when he tried to prevent him standing as mayor 15 years later.

Today, the left in Britain could be in the ascendant once again, but as part of a very different landscape and type of politics, fuelled not by the politics of 30 years ago but by a Europe-wide social movement against the excesses of neo-liberalism. This has seen a surge in support not just for Labour but for the Green Party, the SNP in Scotland, Syriza in Greece and Podemos in Spain.

Publishing a book which touches on fast-moving political events is always a challenge, and it is important to point out that the three interviews collected here took place in September 2015. This was before Ken was appointed co-chair of Labour's Defence Review, another high-octane role in which he will once again be at the sharp end. His thoughts on the future of Trident and the Defence Review are laid out in Chapter 4. As ever with Ken, since then he has, if not courted controversy, found himself at the centre of it.

Unusually for a politician on the left, Ken has been at the heart of events around old Labour, New Labour and now Jeremy Corbyn's leadership of the Labour Party. While it is impossible to predict what will happen over the next few months and years, it seems clear that Ken's past and present experience is more relevant to the future of left politics than ever before. It has been both timely and fascinating to be a part of this collaboration.

Anna Minton, on behalf of the Left Book Club

Foreword

For the first time in decades the people of Britain have a stark but clear choice about our future. We can re-elect a Tory government that will continue to devastate the public services that gave my generation the best quality of life in human history, or we can elect a Labour government under Jeremy Corbyn that is committed to a fairer society in which everyone can achieve their full potential.

Because the election of Jeremy (by a popular landslide unprecedented in Labour's previous leadership elections) offers us that choice, the corporate elite will do everything in its power to defeat us. The tidal wave of media smears, lies and abuse that Jeremy has had to face is just a sign of what is to come.

Tony Blair's admission that 'I always thought my job was to build on some of the things [Margaret Thatcher] had done rather than reverse them' explains why the 'New Labour' government continued to preside over an increasingly unbalanced economy as the banks grew and our manufacturing base was decimated.[1] The refusal to restart building council homes has created the worst housing crisis since the Second World War, with ordinary families forced to leave the communities they and their parents had lived in for generations.

In this book my account of the poisonous 2012 mayoral election is a warning of what will be thrown at Labour in the run up to the 2020 election. Jeremy knows that the five tax-dodging billionaires who own most of our newspapers will do everything they can to prevent Labour getting across its alternative economic strategy. This is why he will restore democracy and open up debate in the Labour Party, creating a campaigning mass movement similar to that which elected the 1945 Labour government and changed our lives for the better.

My co-authors interviewed me about my time with the GLC and as Mayor of London to show what can be achieved by a Labour Party that offers a real choice. But don't just read this book. Get involved. Be part of building the movement that we need to win the next election and give our children and grandchildren the opportunities that we took for granted.

Ken Livingstone, December 2015

CHAPTER ONE

The GLC Years

Ken Livingstone in Conversation with Anna Minton

Let me take me you back, if I may, to May 1981, when you'd recently been elected, at just 35 years old, to one of the most important jobs in London government, as leader of the Greater London Council (GLC). It was also a time of huge turbulence for the left. A few months later, in September, the left-wing candidate Tony Benn would challenge Denis Healey for the deputy leadership of the Labour Party and lose by the slimmest of margins, gaining 49.6 per cent of the vote to Healey's 50.4 per cent. Had Tony Benn won that election the history of the left may have looked very different…

I suppose if you'd been interviewing me then, I would have said that by now I'd assume we'd be living in a social democratic paradise. Because at that point, when we won the election to the GLC, the Thatcher government was deeply unpopular and there was no certainty that she'd be re-elected.

What I felt particularly strongly at the time was the example of history – what had been done in London in the past, in terms of setting the stage for the post-war welfare state. When Herbert Morrison won the London County Council in 1934 he broadly used it as a test bed for the welfare state that the then Labour government brought in in 1945. And I specifically felt that the things we were doing there, after all the disappointments of the Wilson-Callaghan government – that these were a chance to set a new agenda and to win that ideological debate for the left. Wilson and Callaghan had just so abysmally failed to reset – nothing like as bad as Blair of course – so they [the left] were looking for somebody else to go on and do this.

People have talked about how you tried to revive democracy and democratic processes during your time at the GLC. I've read that there were meetings that would have 30, 40 people packed into the room and that it felt like it was just a completely different style of doing things.

Under the old Labour administration, even when we were in opposition, there was a line – you got your whip every Friday afternoon telling you how you had to vote for the next week and there'd be discipline if you broke the whip and all that. But I just said from the beginning: 'This is how we'd like you to vote but it's up to you how you vote. It's a matter between you and your local party or constituents.' And the rebellions just didn't happen. People felt that everything was being openly and honestly discussed in the Labour group. My committee chairs were free to oppose a policy that the leaders' committee had agreed when they got to the group meeting, so it was a very open democratic structure. With the exception of the fiasco over rate capping, I don't think we ever really lost a vote on anything.

Given we only had a majority of four, it was an awful lot of just day-to-day management, of needing to be in the building and around and talking to people. When I was mayor it was a much more executive role, but this was about managing the group – holding it together. We'd won 50 seats, the Tories 41, and the Liberals had one, and then two defected. So we went from a majority of eight down to four. And there were eight members who really couldn't stand me and who'd have been happy to see me replaced. So, just holding it all together and managing it was important.

Can we talk a bit about the culture of the GLC – the idea of the 'People's Palace' and the very different sort of culture and style of government you had there?

Well it had become this nightmarish bureaucracy. If you look back at Herbert Morrison's London County Council – Morrison was leader between 1934 and 1940 and became deputy prime minister under Clement Atlee – it was quite innovative and open. But then there was a succession of bureaucratic Labour leaders right the way up to 1965 when the LCC was replaced by the GLC. The whole thing was structured around the traditional civil service and bureaucracy and so opening it up was electrifying. But some of the senior officers had doubts. Six, seven weeks in, the head of personnel went to see the medical officer and demanded to be declared unfit for work so he could retire immediately. And he did this on a Friday night, so we came in on the Monday and the whole HR side had just gone. But we were really lucky because Maurice Stonefrost, who was the Treasurer, was quite enthused by all of this.

He emerges as quite a key figure and he became pivotal to the way you ran the GLC.

He was a really nice guy to work with. If he'd been the sort of hostile bureaucratic type he could have made our lives so difficult, given that he controlled the entire financial side of things. But he did everything possible to make sure we could carry our policies through.

I read somewhere that in one of your really large meetings a woman actually changed her baby's nappy, which provoked outrage from some of the Tory elders.

Oh yes. No one would really notice that now. Same with homosexuality. This was a time when even though it was no longer illegal, anyone in public life who was exposed as gay had to resign their seat in Parliament immediately, or someone like Dusty Springfield had to go through their entire life living a lie and so on. And raising issues like lesbian and gay rights, or Ireland, this was all just off the agenda. I think that part of the failure of the Kinnock Labour Party was that he just wasn't in touch with the changes that were starting to come up through society. He was traditional Labour from South Wales and all the people around him thought this was completely diversional – just stuff about women, lesbians, gays, blacks. They said, 'let's stick to traditional working class stuff'. They didn't realise that our society was undergoing a huge change.

And why do you think you did realise that, despite also being quite enmeshed in Labour Party politics?

Basically I was young. I'd grown up in London which had waves of immigration which changed us. But also my background wasn't in politics. My interests as a kid were astronomy and natural history and my first eight years in work were spent as a technician in cancer research. It meant I came to politics with a mind based on scientific research, in which to find the truth you examine the data. Whereas for most people in politics, it's like a matter of faith. And if the facts don't conform to their preconceptions they tend to ignore them. And so I was open to new ideas. I'm still very nerdy and obsessed and read the science stories in the papers first.

You were very much trying to set up a 'real' left alternative, after all the accusations that Labour before 1979 had been 'in office but not in power'. So what were the key planks of your programme?

The key one was transport because at the time we were in a quite deep recession. You always got a seat on the tube, even in the rush hour, and there were an awful lot of empty seats. And we felt that by cutting the fares it was a way of getting people out of their cars and onto public transport. And also it's a way of putting money back in people's pockets. It's redistribution. Then again, I'd never driven – I'd like to see us all in a public transport world.

Why did you never drive?

Because it was so expensive basically. I remember I took some driving lessons in 1967 and each lesson was about the equivalent of a fifth of my weekly pay, and then even when you did have a car there were parking charges and all that. So the commitment to public transport was actually a way of redistributing a bit of wealth to people. We had to increase the rates to cut the fares, but 60 per cent of our rates came from the business sector and half of that from the giant corporations in the City of London and Westminster, so it was a rough and ready but very good mechanism for redistributing wealth.

How about the other parts of your programme, such as industry and employment?

When we were drawing up the manifesto for the 1981 election, we aimed to work out exactly how we were going to pay for everything, so we went into the election with the aim – actually an incredibly big aim – of being able to pay for it. And the biggest single chunk of that was the industry employment side of it. But when it came to carrying it out, I left that completely to Mike Ward[1] – it was his area of expertise. I was quite good at delegating. That's why the GLC worked. Compared to the nightmare of Blair's New Labour where everything was one-to-one meetings, we actually had a proper cabinet structure so that all the committee chairs met every week – I think it was Tuesday mornings – and everything was discussed, every idea that came up was tested and argued over and so on. There was no sort of thing of me announcing 'we're doing this' or 'we're doing that' and that's the first people heard of it.

I talked to Doreen Massey,[2] who worked with you at the Greater London Enterprise Board,[3] and she said that it was an incredible time because it was about trying to counter the coming financialisation of the economy and the Tory plans for deregulation.

Honestly, the Greater London Enterprise Board never achieved as much as we wanted because the powers of the GLC were quite limited. You had to work by building a consensus with business organisations, but I think Mike Ward has said he doesn't think he ever had a meeting with any of the City finance corporations. We were looking at workers co-ops and things like that and trying to rebuild our manufacturing base. Patrick Abercrombie's post-war plan had included a commitment to reduce London's population to 5 million by 1990.[4] So in that first 25 years after the war they were moving all the people out to new towns and moving jobs out. When Labour was elected in 1973 we stopped that because it was hollowing out London and it didn't work.

But at the same time, public transport had been neglected because of this idea that one day everyone would have a car. The plan at the time we won the 1973 election was that all the great motorways would come into central London so that the

M1 would come into Hyde Park, the M23 would come straight up through West Norwood, through Brixton, then you'd have these three concentric ringways, so we'd have looked like some absolutely ghastly American city. So the 25 years we'd had of people working slowly towards better public transport would fade out and everyone would have their own car. We realised this was going to be devastating for London, so the GLC election in 1973 was about a shift away from that. We ran on a commitment to oppose the motorways and therefore you had to rebuild public transport.

Let's talk about Ireland now and how you became interested in the Republican cause.

I remember watching the first non-unionist MP in the '60s being interviewed on TV and explaining just how great the degree of discrimination was there. So, in the late '60s, before the armed struggle started, I saw that what was being done to Catholics in Northern Ireland was similar to what happened to black people in the Deep South in America – it was the same pattern of discrimination. Once the bombing campaign had started and I was selected to stand for Hampstead [in 1977] – well, Hampstead starts in Kilburn and suddenly I'm in the biggest Irish community in London. So, then I started getting involved as Irish groups were coming to see me. The majority of Irish just wanted to keep their heads down because there was an awful lot of violence and hatred directed at them. But I had started reading about Ireland and I'd got a sense of what we'd done over the years. I realised this was just wrong.

I covered Northern Ireland as a journalist in the mid 1990s and when I went there I was just amazed really. I'd done history at school and university – modern history – and I knew something about Ireland. But when I got there, I felt I'd had no idea. I realised 'this is Britain's war', and it felt like no one had really told us. To what extent do you think it was that very partial reporting of the politics of Northern Ireland that meant most people weren't really aware of what was going on?

The Thatcher line was that this wasn't political, these were just psychopaths and criminals. My first visit to Northern Ireland must have been in early 1982 and I remember being really shocked, it was like going back to Britain in the 1950s, it was just so poor and so drab. And at that stage Sinn Féin was saying that the IRA can never defeat the British Army, that there has to be a political solution. And oddly enough, years later, when I used to get invited down to the army training college at Camberley, the officers there would say, 'we always knew we couldn't defeat the IRA. Every time we killed one there would be ten more recruits.' It had to be a political solution. And this was in the mid 1990s, before Blair did the deal. After I'd spoken to the army officers, there would be a unionist on the platform and they [the officers] would tear them apart saying, 'you have got to make concessions – our people are being killed because you're just being so stubborn'. But the idea that this was the view of leading figures in the armed forces never came across at all.

When I came back from that meeting [in 1982] we said that there's potential here to do a deal and end the conflict. But Thatcher just continued, completely obdurate. And another 1,000 people died in the years leading up to Blair's deal, completely unnecessarily.

In 1983, you and Jeremy Corbyn invited Gerry Adams and Danny Morrison to the House of Commons.

Because Jeremy had just been elected as an MP, we had a meeting in the House of Commons. The point was to get across that these people weren't psychopaths and gangsters. And there was overwhelming hostility from the media of course. But Jeremy and myself both recognised that you had to have that negotiated deal otherwise we'd just be locked into decades and decades of violence. It's just sad that Thatcher didn't wake up to that between us inviting Adams to London and Blair's peace deal.

Why was Thatcher so unable to see that?

You've got to remember that the Tory Party used to be also based in Northern Ireland as well as in Britain. All the Democratic Unionists and the Ulster Unionists, they were part of the Tory Party in the old days. And even when Thatcher went, John Major couldn't do anything because he didn't have a majority big enough to survive and he needed those Ulster Unionist votes to prop his government up. It was only when you had Tony Blair there with a huge majority that they could put together that package.

But it was really John Major who started the discussions wasn't it?

Yes, but he excluded Sinn Féin, that was the problem. It was a complete waste of time basically. You've got to deal with the people who are doing the fighting or there's no point.

Given the time, it was politically a very brave stance for you to take. You must have had Special Branch and MI5 crawling all over you.

Oh yeah. My phone's bugged all the time. But the thing is, I didn't see it as brave, I saw it as telling the truth. All the way through my career people have said to me, 'why did you say that?' And I would say, 'because it's true', and they'd say, 'that's not the point'. But I've always thought that is exactly the point.

But it's scary having your phone bugged, isn't it?

No. I don't say anything in private that I'm not prepared to say in public really.

You just don't seem to have that fear that many people might have had, sticking your neck out on issues that seemed politically beyond the pale.

The only thing I had a fear of was failing. That was my worry. And that my generation of politicians are leaving a much worse world than we were given. I don't fear my opponents are going to try and destroy me.

But I wasn't prepared for the wave of what came, because up until I became the leader, coverage of the GLC was negligible. Then the *Daily Mail* brought this guy back from covering the war in the Middle East and he was told to file six stories a day. He was a bag of nerves – he was put under such pressure. It was just unbelievable the scale of it.

This was at a time when I was completely demonised – about everything. The *Mail* had this line about how when we cut the fares it was the first step towards a Soviet economy – all that stuff.

Throughout the first six months I was leader I put myself forward to all the newspapers for interviews and it was just a complete waste of time. They just lied. The line from Tory central office, working with the *Mail* and the *Telegraph* and the others, was to depict us all as basically pro-Soviet traitors to Britain. Because having defeated the Argentines, the next struggle was against the enemy within.

And that's what it was, wasn't it – it was just a line?

The idea that somebody like me would be pro-Soviet, under Brezhnev was ... well ... just ridiculous.

With the benefit of hindsight, it seems like it was political calculation and strategy on the part of the Tories to portray you as an extremist and say 'don't vote for these people, you'll be voting for a Soviet economy'.

But it's exactly what they're doing to John McDonnell and Jeremy Corbyn now as well. Half the interviews I've done about them recently are about what one of them said 20 or 30 years ago, rather than focusing on the economic strategies they're now putting forward. Now they're depicting Jeremy as a threat to national security, and people's homes and jobs and all of that.

You knew Jeremy Corbyn and John McDonnell pretty well during your time at the GLC, didn't you?

I've known Jeremy since the early '70s. He got on Haringey Council in '74, I got on Lambeth in '71, and then we were always involved in campaigns together. He was a key player in the campaign to get a left-wing GLC and I always said 'come on the GLC with us', but he went for the parliamentary seat in Islington North.

Were you friends?

Oh yes. I didn't see too much of him once I became mayor because I got caught up completely in all that stuff and I gave up my seat in Parliament. There were so many issues in Parliament we were both campaigning on together. I've just been sorting out all my old files and throwing a lot away and there's lots of joint Jeremy-Ken Early Day Motions and letters and things like that. I think the only disagreement I've had with Jeremy over these last 40 years was on whether we should intervene in Kosovo.

What's he like?

He's a really nice guy. I've never seen him lose his temper or be rude to anyone. You couldn't say that about me! And I think that's what connects with people – he just comes over as a nice, regular guy, as opposed to all these elites like Blair and the New Labour lot who ended up living in an unreal world, cut off from ordinary people.

And of course John McDonnell was very much at the GLC with you.

Oh yes. I met him in 1981, when he got selected. And he was my deputy leader after the first or second year. Every year he produced a balanced budget, no borrowing. Real grasp of details.

To go back to the media campaign against you, some of your Labour group didn't like all the headlines that you were generating.

Well it was a real shock. I remember a guy from *Time Out* came to interview me in the early '80s and he said he'd been to the press files at one of the Fleet Street papers, and there were more stories on me than on anyone else except Margaret Thatcher. It was just overwhelming. The fabrications were amazing – that Gaddafi had given me £200,000 in a Swiss bank account and all that. I remember my mum phoning me up to say 'why have you had a vasectomy?' It was in the paper!

I wanted to talk about the nuclear free zone. As someone who grew up in London in the 1980s, that really jumped out – that there really was this absurd government advice about what to do in the event of a nuclear attack.

What's interesting was that the GLC was very much run like a traditional civil service. We weren't allowed to just go and rummage through the files. You had to ask for specific documents. And the civil defence department inside the GLC was filled almost completely with people who had come from the ministry of defence and who were totally hostile.

We had to bring in Duncan Campbell, the journalist. We appointed him, so he was on the staff, so he could access the files. And what he brought out was this stunning stuff about all the crap the government was telling you – that you should hide under your table and come out after a couple of days. The plan was, the military would ring all the major cities and

1.1 *Keep London out of the Killing Ground.* Peter Kennard. GLC peace poster 1983.

shoot anyone trying to leave. Because they believed there was a chance you could sustain the non-urban population, post-nuclear war. So we started broadcasting all this stuff and they hated it.

There's some interesting stuff written up about the panics inside the government as we started publishing all this. They were talking about trying to prevent it leaking and all that, and in the end they couldn't do anything. And of course a couple of years later you had the discovery of the extinction of the dinosaurs by a comet and then the recognition that, following a nuclear war, no one's actually going to survive. It's going to be millions of years before life really recovers and repopulates the planet. And yet we've still got the idea now of buying more nuclear submarines, which is just bizarre.

I couldn't believe the advice saying, 'keep a bucket of water on each floor, there will be a short period before fallout descends, use this time to do essential tasks'. It's just ludicrous.

And of course, the other thing was that the leader of the GLC was supposed to be whisked to the royal bunker along with the cabinet, somewhere in Essex, while a military commander was appointed to oversee London. I'd be able to advise, but only advise – he was in charge. And so we published all this stuff. But I don't think most people ever became aware of it really. I remember Illtyd Harrington, my deputy, was barred from standing as an MP in 1964 because he was in CND. In those days, George Brown, who was deputy leader of the Labour Party, and Sara Barker, Labour Party National Agent, would go out for lunch with MI5 officials who'd been given a list of all the newly selected Labour candidates, and they'd then be told who they should stop from standing. So MI5 was given a veto. Not many were stopped, but all this stuff was so outrageous.

We unveiled our first great big poster somewhere down in Streatham and what was interesting was that the majority of Conservative voters thought we should be a nuclear free zone in London, which came as a surprise.

It seems that puncturing the media mythology was suddenly very effective. But you also had a lot of flak about all the grants that you gave out.

And this shows you what was wrong with Kinnock. In the '87 election Labour had no commitment to reinstate a regional authority for London. By 1992 they realised they should, but one of the clauses in the manifesto said 'the new authority will have no freedom to give grants to anybody' (*laughs*). The level of controversy about this is hard to believe now, particularly when I think something like three quarters of our grants went to things like children's playgroups.

Well I've got the figures here: women's centres and playgroups £29 million; lesbian and gay groups £5 million; peace groups £1.5 million; police monitoring groups £6 million. And you gave almost £80 million to housing repairs, just before you left the GLC. So it's not exactly a controversial list is it? I mean, Labour's Sure Start policy drew a lot from that didn't it?

If you could have a time machine and take people forwards and say well, here's a Conservative prime minister allowing gay marriage and here's a Labour Party setting up preschool childcare and all that – we were just ahead of our time that was all.

What I'm interested in is what it was that made you ahead of your time? Was it a function of being in London?

No, no. Look at other leaders in London. The thing about me is that I've always had an open mind. People come to you with a good idea – supporting kids' playgroups, whatever it might be, and I do it.

Looking back, it jumps out at me that you said things that were so unexpected of a politician. You said you weren't going to the Royal Wedding[5] and you told the People's March for Jobs, 'you can come and sleep on camp beds in my office', after 500 unemployed people marched 280 miles from Liverpool to London.

The People's March for Jobs was brilliant because they actually crossed the boundary into London the day of our first council meeting when we formally took control. And so we all went up there to meet them at the Harrow border and then we rushed back and they arrived later on in the afternoon. We had all these camp beds which were set aside in the event of the nuclear war. So we had a lot of room.

Then there's the story about the journalists who were striking at Time Out. *They came to you and you gave them a loan to set up a new magazine.*

I don't see anything particularly shocking about that. It was much better to have two magazines than one.

Let's move on to some of the big controversies surrounding your time at the GLC. It's clear that some of the key issues chime directly with the contemporary history of the left more widely, in that all these battles are well known to anyone who is politically aware and over 50, but barely known at all to those under 40, particularly those who may not follow politics quite so closely. For example, the whole idea of a caucus, or the crisis in the Labour Party over rate capping – these were seminal issues for the future of the left but most young people today would struggle to know what they were about. Can you tell me about the caucus which brought you the Labour leadership?

Once Labour lost the GLC in 1977, bizarrely I was the only lefty not to lose their seat. Tony Banks lost his seat at Feltham and had he kept it he would have been the candidate for Labour leader. People had barely heard of me and between '77 and '79 I struggled to get any interest in what was happening at the GLC. And then after, I think it must have been late '79, there was a lefty conference up at Hampstead Town Hall. I had booked to have a thing about what can we do with the GLC and no one came – I was the only person in the room.

When we lost the GLC election in 1977 we went from having 58 Labour members to just 28. It was really only in the 12 months before the 1981 election that lots of people started turning up. The thing was to encourage young people to stand and to have new people coming in. We had a huge wave of new people coming in. Andrew McIntosh, who became the leader of the Labour group in 1980, could easily have brought Illtyd Harrington and Harvey Hines, the chief whip, on board, but it was clear he was going to be a real disaster [as leader] because he would just meet with the officers and he wouldn't even include his deputy or his chief whip. And he wouldn't even have his chief of staff in the room. And so everyone said, 'how's it going to be, he can't run the thing like this'. Whereas I was open and inclusive, and so the centre ground supported me. Without them I wouldn't have won.

Can you just explain, so people can understand, what does a caucus mean?

People talk about the democrat caucus in the American Congress – it's all the democrat members turning up once a week to discuss things. I think we should just call them meetings. Caucus suggests something sinister. But they are just meetings. But the left caucus, everyone knew it was there.

I looked it up, as I wanted to understand. Although the definitions vary, this is one of the clearer definitions I could find: 'a group or a committee within a group, attempting to determine policy through voting together'.

That's a good description of it. The caucus which elected me leader of the GLC was open to anyone who wanted to come.

This was also in the context of the massive struggle between left and right within the Labour Party, just months before the election for deputy leader between Tony Benn and Denis Healey. You were trying to take the GLC to the left – this was what it was all about, wasn't it?

It was the wave of anger unleashed as a result of Callaghan's failure. It's a bit like what has been unleashed for Corbyn, with this surge of people joining their constituency Labour Parties and the campaign to say the leader should be elected by an electoral college, not just the MPs and all that. They were great times, it just took a little while to get people interested in how the GLC might do something in all of this.

To get back to the caucus, Mrs Thatcher massively used this didn't she? It was one of the planks of the attack on you. And it became one of the planks of the attack on the Labour Party – the concept of the block vote.

But everywhere in politics people sit around and plot. I'm sure that Mrs Thatcher sat around with all her close colleagues plotting against the majority of her Cabinet who didn't agree with her. That's just life in politics.

I agree. But it sits uneasily with democratic processes doesn't it?

Well we don't have a very participatory democracy. We just get a vote every now and then. And people get elected and left to get on with it.

Do you think that we should have a more participatory democracy?

I've been in favour of proportional representation since the mid '70s, but I think democracy in this country has got worse and worse. You've got a Tory government that's got a majority in Parliament but only 25 per cent of the population voted for them. And 25 per cent didn't bother voting at all. And the other 50 per cent voted against them. I think that should be reflected in Parliament. But you would very seldom get a majority government and it would mean Labour would have to work with Greens, and the SNP and the Lib Dems on occasion.

Let's talk about Fares Fair and the famous court case, where your low fares policy was overturned.

The GLC had the power to set fares. But the Law Lords ignored that and they went back to the 1950s – there'd been a clause in local government which said you should always try and not spend too much, or something like that. And they revived this after 30 years and imposed it. But the anger about this was such that about a year later, my head of law came to see me saying he'd been informed that if we wanted to cut fares again then as long as we did it in a slightly different way the judges wouldn't overrule it. So clearly the judges realised they'd ****ed up.

So basically the Law Lords overruled your Fares Fair policy.

I think because they felt we were this dangerous security risk and they should do something to try and stop us. It was the most biased political judgement I've been aware of in my political lifetime. It just completely ignored the law and it caused a huge backlash. There were all these campaigns – people dressing up as judges and getting on buses and things like that.

I'd like to talk about rate capping now. I was only vaguely aware of this, and didn't realise until now what rate capping was about – that the Tory government was trying to limit the amount councils could charge through the rates and that a number of Labour authorities were opposing what they saw as an assault on spending. Looking back on this almost a generation later, and with so much of the story obscured by political rhetoric and point scoring, it does seem complicated.

It wasn't. It was a Conservative measure to stop councils raising money to spend on services – that was at was the core of it. It was about centralising power and smashing local democracy.

But what is complicated is how it actually panned out. You then had a number of Labour councils who decided to defy the measure. Can you explain that?

We had a coalition of councils put together who said they would not set the budgets that the government had imposed on them. But the problem we had was that by law the GLC had to set a budget by a fixed time in February, whereas county councils and borough councils could put it off until June, as Lambeth did. So we were faced with the deadline first and I only had a majority of four. And we had no chance of being able to defy Thatcher on that because at least eight Labour Party members wouldn't vote to break the law. So we had this nightmare two days of meetings in which we lost every single vote.

It got to the point where had that budget not been passed, we would have broken the law and any councillor who hadn't voted for the budget would have been at risk of being prosecuted. A lot of Labour members came to me and said 'look, if you can't get the rate cap budget through, we're going to end up having to vote for the Tories' even smaller one'.

But this is what happened isn't it? In Lambeth and in Liverpool, Labour councils broke the law and were fined hundreds of thousands of pounds.

Yes, and they were barred from office.

They were fined £105,000 in Lambeth and £106,000 in Liverpool. And this has always been portrayed as the fault of profligate Labour councils, but it was essentially a strategy to defy the cuts wasn't it?

Yes. Thatcher was trying to make further massive cuts in spending by local authorities and we were opposed to that. Fortunately for Liverpool and Lambeth, they had sufficient Labour majorities so they could go right down to the wire. But even then, they lost.

You wrote about this in some detail in your autobiography and I've read the other accounts of it as well. I was surprised to hear that Margaret Hodge was one of the councillors who proposed the setting of illegal budgets.

That was 30 years ago – she has changed.

Was there a strategy around the country for Labour councils to fight against the Conservative cuts?

Yes. I didn't lead on this as I was leading the campaign against the abolition of the GLC. John McDonnell led on it and they had regular meetings of those councils, from all over the country, to discuss how they'd manage it and how they'd resist it. If the miners' strike hadn't collapsed the week before, if the miners had carried on, this could have been another big dimension and it might have forced the government to back down. But the collapse of the strike totally dispirited us all.

You had a big fallout with John McDonnell. Can you explain why?

We had those two days of voting on motion after motion after motion to set a rate and all of them were defeated. We got to that last afternoon – I think it was about six o'clock on a Sunday. And as I said, several Labour right-wingers came to me and said, 'if we don't vote to set the rate cap budget, we will have to vote for the Tories' alternative which is even smaller'. I said, 'if that's the case, it's better to go for the rate cap budget than end up with the smaller one'. John McDonnell didn't agree with that, so we were voting on different sides in that one.

You've said in your biography that 'night after night, I couldn't sleep as I tried to work out how we had screwed up so spectacularly. The stakes were so high that John had no qualms in exaggerating the scale of the cuts in order to open a second front against Thatcher. Had they succeeded Thatcher would have been weakened or even defeated and they might have changed the course of recent British history, but the miners' strike collapsed the moment John could no longer hide the truth about the relatively generous Jenkin budget.'[6] So clearly there was a disagreement between you. But it was also something you were massively upset about.

1.2 The final vote on setting the rate (the council tax of the time). County Hall, March 1985. From left to right: Mark Ward, Ken and John McDonnell. Photo: John Chapman.

It was I should imagine the biggest screw up of my political career.

And you and John fell out. I read that he said, 'well Ken is a friend and I don't want to say anything against him, but there is no doubt that he has betrayed the whole campaign in order to save his political career. ... He is a Kinnock.'[7]

But then ten years later, he was there, heading up my campaign to be Mayor of London, so we all got over it and put it behind us.

How did you get over it?

Well, just with passage of time. He got elected to Parliament in '97. We were always on the same side again after that.

Can you tell me a little bit about him, what he's like?

I think he must have been 30 when he got elected as a councillor, something like that. And he just thought it was absolutely wild what was going on at County Hall and he loved it. And I realised he had real abilities so voted to get him elected to be chair of my finance committee, and he was brilliant at it. Every budget he produced was balanced, there was no borrowing and he showed real attention to detail. He became my deputy leader, and if it hadn't been for rate capping we would never have fallen out.

Let's talk about the abolition of the GLC and the campaign to save it, which was such a big focus for you. I was really interested to read that as early as 1981 a lobby group backed by a significant number of major companies, including Cadbury's, Taylor Woodrow, Blue Circle, Sainsbury's and others, were fundraising for the abolition of the GLC. They raised £200,000 for a right-wing group called Aims of Industry to organise a campaign for abolition. So from the moment you got there, they were trying to get rid of you.

Yes. The Aims of Industry group was at the forefront of the neoliberal agenda, and they'd been pushing it for years: small state, low taxes, big profits. And they most likely did genuinely think that we were a threat to the Thatcher agenda so they raised this money to get rid of us. David Sainsbury, now Lord Sainsbury, who was Sainsbury's Finance Director at the time, became a key funder of the Labour Progress Group. And I think, in exactly the same way that he was quite prepared to use Sainsbury's money to abolish the GLC, he provided hundreds of thousands of pounds to set up this Blairite group to try and move the Labour Party to the right.

How did you find out about that 1981 meeting and the threat from Aims of Industry?

It was all over the front page of the *Evening Standard*. Actually, I remember in one of the briefing papers I did for our candidates in the run up to the GLC election I said that there was a very real risk that the Tories may try to abolish the GLC. There were quite a few Tory voices in favour of abolishing it even before I got there.

The other thing that surprised me was the local government bill which proposed not just getting rid of the GLC but the metropolitan county councils as well – so removing a whole level of democratic representation – which is shocking.

It's not shocking. The Tories aren't committed to democracy – they're committed to preserving the world for a small elite.

But there is a democratic strain within Conservatism isn't there?

There isn't. Look how much they welcomed Pinochet, who overthrew a democratically elected government and tortured and murdered thousands of citizens. The Tories have propped up the Saudi Arabian regime with arms and everything else. Tory governments and Republican governments, and sadly often Labour and democrat governments, have supported vicious regimes all over the world.

But there were Tories who were very much against the abolition of the GLC, like Ted Heath.

Yes, we got Ted Heath and quite a lot of others on board. Not many in the House of Commons, but quite a lot in the House of Lords and it was very tight.

1.3   *Say No To No Say*. Anti GLC abolition poster 1984. Agency: BMP; Art Director: Peter Gatley; Copywriter: John Pallant.

Looking back it seems that abolishing the GLC was really a mistake of Mrs Thatcher's, wasn't it?

The simple fact is that if the Tories had ignored me when I became leader of the GLC, if Thatcher hadn't abolished the GLC, there would be none of these books and you wouldn't be interviewing me. I would have just been another local government person who eventually became a backbench MP. It would have been the same if Blair had ignored me when I was running for mayor. So much of my reputation has been created by my enemies.

But do you not think that you were a very effective communicator of the message that the left of the Labour Party was trying to get across in the earlier part of the 1980s? There was a very significant left movement at the time, led by Tony Benn, but you were one of the key players in it, and that's why they went for you.

That's why the media demonised me. But it was the abolition of the GLC – and it was the same with Blair's attempt to prevent me running for mayor – that made me immensely popular again.

I read that the former Conservative environment secretary Patrick Jenkin met you in 2000 and congratulated you on becoming mayor, and you replied, 'Oh Patrick, you made it all possible.'[8] *And in your biography you quote Ted Heath accusing Jenkin of turning 'Livingstone, who was effectively a left-wing nut, into a folk hero'. Do you really think it was the abolition of the GLC that transformed you into the political figure you went onto become?*

The wave of press hysteria had pushed my poll ratings down to about 18 per cent in the autumn of 1981. And then slowly, gradually, by the time we got to abolition it had gone up. There was a majority in favour of all our policies amongst Londoners, except on lesbian and gay rights, and I think that was 44 per cent. We consistently kept pushing the line and it got across to people. And in the opinion polls that were done about what would have happened if Thatcher hadn't cancelled the 1985 election to the GLC, it showed us winning about 90 per cent of the seats. I should imagine it would have been closer in the end, but we were headed for the biggest Labour landslide in London's history, and so Thatcher just cancelled the election.

Which was a phenomenal thing to do, and I think a political mistake of hers.

Well, as I say, if they'd just ignored me … In a sense I was created because of that Tory strategy of the enemy within, and we're under threat and all that, and then again by Blair reviving it all in 1999.

So you fought the abolition of the GLC, with your successful 'Say No to No Say' campaign, which the majority of Londoners supported. And after the House of Commons voted narrowly in favour of abolition, you almost won in the House of Lords, but not quite. Did you ever believe you might win?

We thought we might just pull it off. And if we could have pushed the vote for earlier that day, before everyone got back from Ascot and the races, we might have just made it. That's why the Tories strung out the debate until all the lazy peers who'd spent the day at Ascot got back.

And then you had this final period where you managed to transfer £80 million for housing repairs and you transferred the land for Coin Street, which arguably was the point at which the transformation of the South Bank began. Can you say a little bit about that?

Coin Street was a prime site which nowadays would have tower blocks all over it, filled with offices or luxury homes. What we wanted there was good council housing that people could live in. We worked with the Coin Street Group and transferred the ownership of the land to them. A similar site, Camley Street Natural Park, had been earmarked for developers and we had a real struggle and just about got it done in time and transferred it to the group that was running it just before abolition, and it's still doing really well today. You need to have a proper balance. I encouraged a lot of major development while I was Mayor and it brought a lot of jobs, but we were always looking for sites for parks and affordable homes – you've got to get the balance right.

You must have been devastated by the GLC's abolition.

No, because I actually warned the left caucus before we took power that there might be a move to abolish it. Some Tories had been talking about getting rid of County Hall for years, and so it wasn't a surprise. We did such damage to Thatcher during that campaign for abolition. We couldn't have brought her down – I think they were all a bit paranoid. But she wasted pretty much the first two years of her second term on this. It made them unpopular, it was brilliant. It never occurred to me that the left would continue to be rolled back. I think almost everybody on the left shared that same view.

You had your final concert at the Royal Festival Hall and it sounds like it was very emotional.

It was, it was amazing.

You gave a speech at the end, and you said: 'I do not believe that anything else that happens to us in our lives will be as rewarding and fulfilling as the years that we have spent in this building.' Do you still think that's true?

Oh yes. Being mayor was great fun, but it was an executive American system and I preferred leading a council and being part of that debate. But Blair was in love with all things American. I suppose we were also at the forefront of the struggle against Thatcher at the GLC, whereas it was different with Blair.

There wasn't a common enemy in the same way?

No, no.

Do you think any other local government or city government has done anything similar to what you tried to do at the GLC?

Herbert Morrison used his control of County Hall in the 1930s to create a test bed for the welfare state and I think Harvey Milk in San Francisco – if he'd become mayor it would have been quite electrifying, if he hadn't been assassinated. He was the first openly gay person elected in America, to any office. He was a member of the city government and then this angry old working-class copper shot both him and the mayor in 1978. There's a wonderful film *The Life and Times of Harvey Milk* which is great.

Thank you.

Additional material provided by Angharad Penrhyn Jones

CHAPTER TWO

The GLA Years and Beyond

Ken Livingstone in Conversation with Anna Minton

We talked earlier about how Thatcher's abolition of the GLC transformed you into a hero in many people's eyes. Tony Blair did the same thing, by trying to block you standing for mayor, but it just increased your popularity.

If my enemies had always ignored me, no one would ever have heard of me. I was turned into a star by Thatcher and then revived by Blair.

Let's talk about the campaign to be mayor. You coined the term the 'Millbank Tendency'.

Yes. Just to annoy them. There's this image of Blair, that he was this lovely wonderful human being floating about the rest of us. But the stuff they did was as bad and squalid as in some very unpleasant regimes. Vote rigging and all of that. For all his crap about how we had to reform the trade unions and do away with the block vote, he got the unions which had a right-wing leadership – the electricians and the engineers – not to allow their members to vote on who the candidates for mayor would be and just vote for Dobson. If they hadn't done that I would have been the Labour candidate.

It was dirty tricks on a massive scale. They broke into your bank account and passed on stories to the media about how you were paying for your oldest son's nursery. They even broke into his mother's bank account.[1]

Yes. I wasn't surprised because I lived on the assumption that everything I was doing was being bugged and monitored all my political career. But I assumed it was MI5. It was annoying to find the Labour Party was doing the same thing. I always said it was Blair who dragged Labour down to the Tory level in terms of lies and distortions. Before Blair the Labour Party broadly was interested in policy. It didn't do a lot of negative campaigning at all. It was all a bit nerdy and worthy. But Blair just took on all the awful smear techniques.

But the more the party tried to stop you the more your support went up.

Yes, I was being overwhelmed on the streets. We had huge crowds turning up at meetings and people embracing me. If he'd just ignored it and let us go ahead with it, there would never have been all this hysterical coverage. He feared I would be able to use City Hall to undermine his administration but sadly I didn't have the powers to do that.

The appalling thing is that 230 Labour Party members in London applied to stand for the London Assembly and the vetting panel excluded 136 on the grounds that they lacked life skills. Anyone who was on the left was barred. That's why the present Parliamentary Labour Party is so right-wing. From 1997 to 2010 you couldn't be selected as a candidate unless you'd been put on Blair's approved list. And the moment Ed Miliband abolished that you actually got new Labour MPs, who were much more likely to nominate Jeremy Corbyn than the old lot.

*You became this lightning rod for all the anger against New Labour.
You have told of how you were in the House of Commons tea room
and Cardinal Hume came up to you and said publicly, in front of
everyone, 'I'm really looking forward to voting for this man next
year.'*

He was surrounded by a group of Catholic MPs and one of
them was Edward Leigh, the Tory, and the look on his face
was absolute horror (*laughs*). But I'd worked with Cardinal
Hume at the GLC when we funded a lot of his work for the
homeless, so we'd had a good relationship going back a long
time. And also I was perceived as one of the first people in
politics to really stand up for the Irish community because of
the battering they were getting from the gutter press. And of
course for Cardinal Hume the bulk of his congregation would
always have been of Irish origin.

*Do you think that there was a culture of corruption which was
responsible for the functioning of New Labour, almost from the
very beginning? The way they had approved lists of candidates
and deselected anyone that didn't fit, or didn't have the right face.*

You saw that with the smearing of Liz Davies. It's why in
the end Blair almost destroyed the Labour Party. Sixty per
cent of members left. Ed Miliband abolished the vetting of
candidates but it was disappointing that he didn't restore
proper democracy to the party conference and the policy
making side of things. Now Jeremy will do that. We'll have a
proper Labour Party again which is open and democratic. I
think Ed Miliband's problem was that he inherited a Labour
Party filled with Blairites in the parliamentary party and he
should have faced them down. He was right to say the Iraq war
was wrong and apologise. But he should have also apologised
for New Labour's economic strategy which was carrying on
Thatcherism.

2.1   *Photo-Op.* kennardphillipps 2005. A collaborative work between
Cat Phillipps and Peter Kennard. As Mayor of London, Ken remained
opposed to the war, even when he was brought back into the Labour Party.
Peter Kennard's *Photo-Op* caught the mood of the time.

*Given that you had so much popular support, why didn't you stay
on as an independent for the 2004 mayoral election? Instead you
wanted to rejoin the Labour Party.*

When Tony Blair asked me in 2003, I said yes because I knew
I'd get a lot out of them. By having me back as a candidate,
they'd have to fund a lot more of the things I wanted. I got £2.9
billion to invest in the transport system, we got total support on
the Olympic Games, police numbers, all those sorts of things.

So there was never a question in your mind about actually whether you might stay out of New Labour?

I applied to rejoin in July 2002 and the NEC had a vote on it and I narrowly lost. The trade unions were solidly behind me but all Blair's supporters voted no. But by the time you got to the following summer, Labour was so unpopular in the polls that I think Blair realised they were heading for their worst local government result in 20 years and about the only high-profile thing they could win would be London if I was their candidate.

You never thought to yourself 'I could be the leader of a new left'?

No. If I'd thought I could create a new socialist party and lead it to a majority in Parliament of course I would have done it. But that wasn't going to happen. I don't know how much my popularity was concentrated just in London. Being mayor was a pretty demanding job and I really didn't have the time to create a new party. If I hadn't given up my seat in Parliament in 2001 I would have stood for the Labour leadership when Blair stood down. I imagine Brown would still have won but he wouldn't have had the coronation unopposed that he had. But there we are, we all make mistakes.

Let's talk about your programme at the Greater London Authority (GLA). Once again, as it had been at the GLC, transport was a central focus. You brought Bob Kylie over from the US and you embarked on a battle with Gordon Brown about 'PPP', which stood for the 'Public Private Partnership' of the tube, later described by commentator Christian Wolmar as 'one of the great scandals of the decade'.[2] Why did you appoint Bob Kylie?

How did it happen? We advertised and he must have applied. And literally from the moment we spoke to him it was clear he had such experience and skills and that's what we wanted to modernise the London Underground – he'd been in charge of modernising the Boston Underground and the New York Underground which are the second and third oldest in the world – and Brown was pushing this ridiculous PPP. Also, given Brown's besotted love of all things American, we thought if we produced Bob Kylie for him he might drop all this PPP crap. But he refused to meet Bob – he wouldn't have anything to do with him.

You are quoted as saying about Kylie, 'I can't believe I'm trying to recruit an ex-CIA agent.'

(*Laughs*) Yes. He had some wonderful stories, because he was personal assistant to the director of the CIA. But he was actually kept out of all the dirty stuff, the assassinations, he was never told about any of that. We got on fine, he was brilliant.

Can you explain PPP in really simple terms – because it seems that every Labour Public Private Partnership became almost impossible to understand. What I'm wondering is, was this similar to the Private Finance Initiative (PFI)?

Yes, but it was also much more complicated because the old bureaucrats at London Underground were hopeless. They completely agreed with Blair's government. You couldn't trust them to do this so that's why we hired Bob Kylie who had a record of modernising undergrounds. But the PPP was even worse than PFI. The contract filled two four-drawer filing cabinets. And if you're drawing up a contract for a 30-year programme of modernising this vast underground system, it's a nightmare of complexity. It was literally just a private finance initiative but it was the biggest and most complex one anyone ever came up with. And every single transport person who looked at it just said, 'this isn't going to work, this is a disaster'.

When I finally managed to get Bob Kylie in for a private meeting with Blair, he had to go down to Chequers because Blair was frightened Brown would go mad if he saw Kylie coming into Downing Street. Kylie took Blair through it and explained it and Blair ended up saying, 'oh yes, it's very worrying'. But Brown wouldn't back off so Blair went along with the plan for PPP.

When Brown became prime minister, the first meeting we had was at the memorial for 7/7. I quietly said to him that the Metronet firm which had control of two thirds of the network was about to go bust and was £1.8 billion in debt and he just said, 'let my office know'. That was the only conversation we ever had about it and they picked up the entire bill, because I wasn't going to. What I find bizarre is that someone with Brown's intelligence was just so prepared to ignore all the advice coming in. Brown is clever. He was sent to university at the age of 15.

But it's not very intelligent to have done all those PFI contracts for hospitals. He seems to have been in love with that sort of financing. It seems to have been an ideological belief in a certain kind of financing which has proved not to work at all.

I know, that's what I find hard to believe, how people don't look at the facts. And we're still picking up the bill.

You also had a battle over the Oyster card, and then there was the congestion charge which was difficult to get through but was quickly a big success. It's obviously something you're very proud of.

The state of congestion in central London was so bad at that stage – something had to be done about it. Singapore had had this scheme running since 1979 and so we adopted it. We had to make sure it worked perfectly from day one, or we'd never have been forgiven. The only thing we underestimated was the number of people that stopped driving in. We thought 20 per cent would stop but it was 40 per cent. Then we extended it to Kensington and Chelsea but Boris reversed that.

The next stage on from the congestion charge was low emissions, so that the whole of London became a Low Emission Zone, and HGVs – Heavy Goods Vehicles – had to pay a charge if they were coming in because of their pollution. But Boris hasn't really developed that. By now we would have reduced diesel vehicles coming in in order to improve air quality. Today congestion is almost back to being as bad as it was when I was elected.

So you looked around the world to find exemplars of how other cities did things.

We also looked at Paris for their bike scheme. In a city like London, if you do something that's a complete first, there's a real risk that if it doesn't work it can be very damaging. It's much better to let smaller cities experiment with something and then take the idea once it's been shown to work. A catastrophic mistake in central London would be global news.

Are you annoyed that the bikes are known as 'Boris Bikes'? Is that irritating, seeing as it was your idea in the first place?

No. It's there, it's working and that's the important thing. Bike ridership had doubled during my mayoralty and it's carried on growing. The annoying thing about Boris is that when he got in he cancelled plans to have separate lanes to physically separate bikes from cars. He scrapped that and just had these blue lanes painted. Now, as the deaths have continued, he's finally brought the idea back and they are putting those in. But he's wasted seven bloody years.

That's quite shocking really, given the amount of cycle fatalities we have in London and given that he's a champion of cycling.

Yep.

I want to ask you about your relationship with the Jewish community. In your autobiography you said that your views on multiculturalism crystallised when you got to know the Orthodox Jewish community as GLC member for Stoke Newington. You wrote: 'Between the Orthodox and the fully assimilated, each Jew has made his own choice, and that is what I want, for all our communities.'

In 1977 I was the GLC Member for Stoke Newington, which has the biggest Orthodox Jewish community anywhere in Europe. I got on very well with them. They were basically poor because so many of the men spend all their time reading religious texts. It will be the same within the Muslim community. In 50 years there'll be some women still wearing the hijab, and others who haven't a clue what's in the Quran. That's the way things go, people make their own choice. As someone who's an atheist, I prefer the non-orthodox choice frankly, but it was interesting to represent that community.

If anything, faith groups are growing stronger all over the world. There's been a revival of religion. I was hoping it would continue to decline, as it did in that post-war period. But now, you've had this real revival with the evangelical Christians in Britain.

Given that representing Stoke Newington was quite a pivotal experience for you in forming your views on multiculturalism, why do you think you've gone on to have such difficult relationships with the Jewish community?

Because I'm a critic of Israeli government policy and the Israel lobby just denounces anyone who criticises their government as anti-Semitic. It's really ridiculous because each time I was elected my first decision was to appoint a Jewish deputy. Each year I was mayor anti-Semitic incidents declined. The moment Boris got in they went up 50 per cent. How do you explain that?

In 2006 when Israel invaded Lebanon, anti-Semitic incidents doubled immediately across Britain and Europe, but not in London – they didn't go up at all. I think that because you had a mayor who was prepared to be critical of Israel, that diminished anti-Semitism.

Your relationship with the Jewish community has been called into question a number of times, but most memorably perhaps as a result of the row with the Evening Standard, *which resulted in you being suspended from office in 2006. Can you explain the events which led up to this?*

The *Evening Standard* had never asked to attend any of the functions we put on, until we put one on for the lesbian and gay community. I said 'you're not coming to that, because you're just going to end up writing lots of snide bits and pieces'. But as I left the building a reporter ran after me shouting questions and I told him to bugger off or something. He said he was only doing his job and I said, 'that was the defence of the concentration camp guards', to which he replied, 'you can't say that to me, I'm Jewish', but how would I know the reporter was Jewish? The *Standard* put a huge effort into building this up as an issue, they got the Board of Deputies of British Jews lined up and they asked the Standards Board for England to sanction me – which has the power to bar you from office for up to five years. They said I should be suspended for four weeks. If they'd suspended me for a day I wouldn't have bothered, but we had to go to the High Court. The judge started by saying: 'I hope no one in this room is going to be alleging that Ken Livingstone is anti-Semitic.' It was an outrageous waste of time and money. The *Standard* under Veronica Wadley was every bit as bad as the *Daily Mail*. And then of course about 18 months later they had Andrew Gilligan writing six months of stories alleging I was corrupt. And they know you can't afford to sue. I remember being told at the time, it will cost £100,000 before you even get to court. Our libel laws have been effectively restructured for the super-rich. It's just appalling. There should have been some sanction or something because it was all completely made up.

Can we talk about housing now? Duncan Bowie, who is a housing academic, was a planner at the GLA between 2002 and 2007. In his book he writes that by the time you came to the GLA, 'the paradigm was fixed and unchallengeable ... [the mayor] had no delivery powers and no ability to raise finance from investment'.[3] Even so I think that he and other critics of yours on the left, such as Doreen Massey who worked with you at the GLC, were disappointed that you weren't able to do more to boost low-income housing in London.

When I became mayor we weren't allowed to have a housing policy. When the mayoralty was created there was a clause that said the mayor would have no responsibilities for housing, education or social services – which is ridiculous. So I actually used planning powers to influence the proportion of affordable housing that had to be provided.

Later, when Blair agreed to give the mayoralty more powers, he agreed the mayor would have responsibility for housing. But this became law just before I lost the election to Boris in 2008. I had got Gordon Brown to agree to give me £5 billion to start building council housing again, but Boris just didn't take it up. So this is the real tragedy of my losing in 2008 – we would have started a proper housing policy which would have grown and grown.

How did you get Gordon Brown to agree to that?

Well, Brown needed me to be a success. He knew that if I lost in 2008 he would be blamed for it. Once I came back into the Labour Party he refused ever to meet me, until he became prime minister. But from then on, although there were occasional backstabbing comments from his press people about me, he knew that he had to make the mayoralty work.

2.2   Ken, Gordon Brown and Nelson Mandela at the unveiling of Mandela's statue in Parliament Square, 29 August 2007.

How many homes would £5 billion have built?

Well it depends. Let me work it out. It would have provided 50,000 homes if we'd been building on land we already owned, and about half that if we'd been building on land we'd had to buy. So between 25,000 and 50,000 homes.

When I came into politics it was all about building more homes, that's what I specialised in – I was vice-chair of housing in Lambeth and chair of housing in Camden. But by the time I became leader of the GLC Thatcher had stopped council house building. We did bits and pieces and John McDonnell got a lot of money out of the GLC at the end to help improve properties and things like that, but of course there was much more focus on the transport side. But I spent a lot of time lobbying Blair to let the mayor have housing powers, and it's disgraceful that Boris hasn't used the £5 billion Brown agreed to.

Boris took me out after the Olympics – the only time we've ever socialised – and I just spent all the time talking to him about house building. I said, you've got to build homes for rent. And he said 'homes for rent' with real shock in his voice. You realise that all these Bullingdon Club Boys have no idea what a housing problem is because they're all given ****ing houses by their parents. It's just appalling.

I know that you made great efforts to use planning powers to get developers to build more affordable housing.

We set out a target. It was 25 per cent when I got in but it was not being enforced. We put it up to 50 per cent. And in my final year we got up to 43 per cent. Then Boris went back to 25 and now any developer turns up and goes to him and says 'we can't afford it', and he's allowing all these schemes to be built without any affordable housing.

Your critics say that you did significantly increase the number of homes being built but that affordable housing did not increase. But, of course, that was in the context of a harsh central government climate towards housing which continued to see more and more council homes sold under Right to Buy and cuts to housing associations which found it increasingly hard to build more social and affordable homes.

We did what we could and we managed, through the planning system, to push the amount of affordable housing developers would provide up to 43 per cent, which was an achievement. I remember that figure really clearly, because I was sitting down and talking to all the developers and always pushing it. Every big development that came to me, we made affordable housing and green space essential to it.

You wrote a candid foreword to Doreen Massey's book, World City,[4] *where you describe how she came to the GLA to interview you when you were mayor and you feared that 'she was about to leap over and bang my head on the table to make the point that "you've got to do more to change it" [the status quo]'. That seems to be an issue that every left leader working within an overarching neoliberal framework has to grapple with.*

Yes. But unless you're sitting there at the leader's desk or the mayor's desk, knowing what you can and can't do, you don't know the scale of the restrictions or the limits on it. What more could I have done that I had the power to do? I did everything it was possible to do. If you've got a clause in a bill that says you have no responsibility for housing, then the only thing you can do is what I did do, which is use affordable housing law through the planning system to drive the figures up – and lobby the government to get powers over housing, and get Gordon Brown to give me £5 billion. It was pretty central to where I wanted to be, and if I hadn't lost the election in 2008 you would now see that City Hall could be a major housing developer.

Let's move on to the Olympics now. You saw it as a potentially important economic gain for London.

My predecessor at the GLC had wanted to bid for the 1988 Olympics but Thatcher wouldn't put the money in. So this idea had kicked around the GLC 30 years earlier. And when the British Olympic Committee came to see me – because you can't bid without the mayor's support – they said they had potential sites in West London or East London and I said I'd support it as long as it was the East London site because there would be this huge legacy benefit.

My recollection is that the Olympic site was completely polluted and had been neglected for yonks. Nothing had been done to it for 30 years. So that was the decision that was made and they stuck to it. We got £8 billion from government, and we'd never have got that without the Olympics. It wasn't so much critics, as people saying we haven't got a chance.

Once we'd won, we then co-operated with Westfield so that their development would be integrated and it would be one big overall development. And of course, the defining thing about that is that people primarily go there by public transport – there are very few cars.

I know that you worked hard to get a good deal for local people, because you signed an agreement with the group London Citizens, to say that there should be a training academy for construction apprentices and that a large percentage of jobs should go to local people. It was a good agreement but the Olympic Delivery Authority ignored it.

I had lost the election by then. Construction only started after I lost. We won the bid in 2005, we spent into 2007 getting a concrete plan together and tying it all down and all of this was built in. But Boris wasn't going to honour it. Unless the mayor's sitting on them these things don't happen. I would have asked for a monthly report on how many people have been recruited from the local area. You set a target like that and it happens. Boris doesn't do stuff like that.

If I'd been elected in 2008, the Olympic Delivery Authority wouldn't have ignored it. That's the problem. The moment I lost, all the things ... the only project that was underway that Boris didn't either dump or put off forever was the bike scheme. Everything else ... we were working out several new tube extensions, DLR extensions, things like that, and he just dropped all of them. And if you lose, there's nothing you can do about it.

To go back to when you won the bid, you were in Singapore, you won and it was a brilliant moment. But the morning after came the London bombings. You talk about that at length later,[5] but I'd also like to mention the wonderful speech you made in Trafalgar Square the following week to the survivors and relatives of those who had died. You quoted Pericles and you said 'in time all great things flow to the city, and the greatest of those is the people who come'. Obviously you've read about city government from the earliest times.

I also read *The Twelve Caesars* by Suetonius when I was at the GLC. Suetonius is wonderful. There's a line about Caesar having meetings on a Friday afternoon because all the rich Senators have buggered off to their estates, and that's exactly what I used to do at the GLC.

That's why I've always loved history – although people think we've advanced massively, actually we tend to go round in cycles, things getting better then worse, then better again. We repeat the same mistakes but also the same successes. Just the technology changes, but an awful lot of things are done the same.

Moving on again, can we talk about Venezuela and your relationship with Hugo Chávez?

We must have had an approach from Chávez's people because he was coming to London and he wanted to meet. And the left groups that were organising his visit had got this big rally at Camden Centre so I chaired it. I thought he was quite a remarkable guy. He spoke for three hours without notes and he was just a normal, unpretentious person. We hit it off perfectly. And he came up with this arrangement – we were giving him advice on how to run a modern transport system and he was paying us a few million pounds which we used to subsidise free travel for the unemployed.

Transport in Caracas is a nightmare and you can spend five or six hours trying to get across the city. It's much worse than here. You were advised if you were driving into Caracas to take a bottle of water, lunch and a book to read. So he wanted help with all that. The Tories all went mad – that we were dealing with a dictator. But Chávez had won all these elections, he wasn't a dictator. And naturally the Americans attempted a coup to get rid of him, which failed. He didn't have a background in politics. He'd been fighting the guerrillas for years and years and suddenly one of his soldiers got shot, he was holding him when he died, and he thought, 'I don't want to be carrying on with this.' And that's what led him to try to and overthrow the old government. He went to prison for a bit and when he came out he won the election. The Americans were furious because he basically nationalised the oil industry.

The agreement with Venezuela was about the first thing that Boris cancelled as soon as he won the election.

It was also you helping out a left-wing government in South America. Were you conscious of that?

Oh yes. I'll help out a left-wing government anywhere. When I went there, my adviser John Ross came with me and we met their finance minister who was also a former guerrilla leader. They were sitting on about £800 billion, just in their reserve. So I was saying, invest it in infrastructure and rebalance the economy, but they never did. The real problem in Venezuela is that petrol is so cheap that everybody has a car, which is a nightmare. I think they wanted to sit on this vast £800 billion because when the oil price goes down it's insurance.

Looking back on your record as mayor, what do you feel you did well and what could you have done better?

Basically, we had to start from nothing. Politicians get elected and they inherit a machine that's been there for centuries sometimes. Here there was nothing and I can't think of any other politician I've ever read about who gets to create the machine. It was great fun and it was very demanding. It's why I gave up my seat in Parliament because of the pressure.

All my key advisers were people I'd been working with politically for ages. John Ross, Neale Coleman, Simon Fletcher and Redmond O'Neal. Neale Coleman has been appointed Jeremy's Head of Policy, which is a very good sign. Most of the first term, apart from the congestion charge, was setting up the system, devising a 20-year economic plan for London and of course just rebuilding the buses. We didn't get the Underground until the end of my first term.

The buses are a big part of your legacy aren't they?

Bus ridership is up 75 per cent over 15 years. I never used to bother waiting for a bus when I was leaving the house to get to the tube. Now one comes by every two or three minutes. Brilliant. If you're going to have a congestion charge and restrict people's ability to drive into the city, you need a viable alternative. There weren't many bus lanes before then. Now, during the rush hour there's this whole line of traffic stretched back but there's the bus able to sail straight on through really quickly. You get there quicker. I am really proud of the bus service, it's a real legacy. But I'm also really proud of the C40 [Cities Climate Leadership Group] which can have a huge impact in terms of tackling climate change.

Can you explain that?

Ten years ago we had 16 mayors come to London – from Beijing, Shanghai, Paris, Moscow... – and we decided to set up what we called the C20, which rapidly became the C40, and now there are about 79 cities involved, which is 10 per cent of the world's population and 25 per cent of the world's GDP. Sixteen of the cities took a decision to retrofit all public buildings to make them energy efficient and Boris has carried on with this to his credit. That doubled the world market for retrofitting in one go, which means that prices have gone down by 40 per cent.

When I lost in 2008, the other mayors weren't prepared to have Boris carry on running it, so they gave it to the Mayor of Toronto, then it moved to Michael Bloomberg in New York and now it's the Mayor of Rio. But Bloomberg did an enormous amount. He built shelters for 2 million New Yorkers for when hurricanes hit and they are forced to flee the Manhattan coastline.

Do you think the buses and the C40 are your main achievements?

Well also the Olympics and its legacy, and the upgrading of the Underground. On the Victoria Line or Jubilee Line a train comes about every one or two minutes. Because it's a very old signalling system, a train would only leave one station as the train was leaving the station ahead of it, but there's been a massive increase in capacity on the lines we upgraded.

If I had to push you and ask you to point to your greatest achievement as mayor, what would it be?

Well, I don't sit around thinking about things like that. The way we handled 7/7 – I don't think there was a single attack on a Muslim in the weeks that followed. I think there's been a significant increase in Islamophobic attacks more recently. But we set the right sort of tone. I suppose I think the biggest legacy is broadly that Boris has not dismantled the structures I left for him. Tony Travers calls him 'Ken Lite'. And if Sadiq Khan or Zac Goldsmith take over next year I doubt if they'll make any significant change either. We got it right.

Going back to how you dealt with 7/7 and the emphasis you've always put on multiculturalism, I wonder if the success of multiculturalism in London is actually one of your greatest achievements?

I don't know if I can claim that – that's a little arrogant. There's a poll that shows that in France 50 per cent of Muslims consider themselves French, whereas here in London 90 per cent consider themselves British.[6] We've done much better at integrating our Muslim community than the French have and I think that has paid off. There's been some erosion of that, because there's been so much Islamophobia from members of this bloody government.

2.3   Bob and Roberta Smith. Painting, donated to Bid for Ken,
Gimpel Fils 2012.

I think that although I've been an atheist since I was 12, and as a teenager I was scathing about religion, I've come to recognise that whether it's Orthodox Jews in Stoke Newington, or Muslims in Willesden, or Catholics, for many people, the framework that defines the way they live is their religion, and therefore I think it's a big mistake to be offensive about religion. It was understanding that those changes were coming, back in the '80s, when most politicians just didn't want to touch any of it.

Going back to your legacy, what do you think you could have done better?

I can't really think of anything I could have done better. My Monday morning meetings with my key advisers were really intense debates. Ideas were floated, a consensus would build up around something, then we could move forward, then we'd have to report back on how it was going. It wasn't like the way New Labour was run, all one-to-one meetings, and no one knew what was going on. It was a really good debate by very bright people. And the reason why congestion charging didn't have any flaws when it started was that we'd done a lot of work to make sure it didn't. We did the same work in defining how the Olympics should be built, although Boris didn't carry on with it for the local community. But no one died in the construction, which has never happened before in the Olympics. We got all the health and safety stuff right. Me and my staff were very good on detail.

That seems to be a big part of your approach to political work, that you actually love the detailed policy stuff. Lots of politicians don't like that, they only like the big picture. But you love the detail.

I think you've got in Jeremy Corbyn someone who's probably a bit like that. Fortunately. I can't see any point in being in politics if you're not going to be doing all of that. You're there to run things – to do things.

You've written a chapter later in this book about Boris, but tell me briefly, how do you see him as a politician?

I think he's a complete waste of space. Apart from being chancellor or prime minister, being mayor is the third best job in British politics and he hasn't done anything. He could have set a complete new right-wing ideological agenda. If you think of my time at the GLC, we were pushing forward in all these new areas. It was the same with my mayoralty. But Boris hasn't done that. He's spent the time promoting himself, writing a couple of books, doing his weekly column for half a million pounds. The whole machine has been geared up to just promoting Boris.

So do you think he's a bit vacuous?

He wants to be there. For Boris, there must be some deep insecurity. He wants to be elected and loved and to be prime minister. But if he ever becomes prime minister, nothing will happen either.

He's an amazing political celebrity isn't he? You were the first political celebrity, and he's bigger than you were.

Yes, but I never wanted to be a celebrity, I just wanted to do the bloody job.

I think you are an incredibly good media performer, and perhaps that's a talent you didn't know you had. Boris has it as well.

I don't think it's a particular talent. I just answer the bloody questions so the interviews are worth looking at.

There's more to it than that.

Well no, I don't think there is. If you look at how bored people were with the Labour leadership debate until Jeremy entered the race – the three other candidates weren't saying anything, everything was calculated – it was deadening.

I think what I'm trying to say is that some people are better at dealing with the media than others. Some people get tongue tied and some people don't express themselves very well.

Mainly it's because they're frightened to say anything that might be controversial.

Just finally on Boris – as a person – how did you find him at that dinner?

He was perfectly pleasant, but mainly he just wanted to ask why I hadn't become prime minister. I think he was hoping that if I told him all the mistakes I'd made to prevent me becoming prime minister, he'd avoid making them himself. That was his main interest, how it was that I didn't get to be prime minister.

Did you tell him what you thought?

Yes. In 1988 Neil Kinnock introduced this rule change which meant that you couldn't stand for leader of the Labour Party unless you were nominated by 20 per cent of MPs.* So that effectively ruled out any serious left-wing challenge until Corbyn was nominated. And Corbyn only got 20 MPs nominating because they agreed with him – the other 15 did it to widen the debate – without that Corbyn couldn't have even stood either.

And now he has won the Labour leadership – that could have been you.

If they hadn't changed the rules. If Kinnock hadn't changed those rules I would have stood against John Smith in '92 and

---

* By 2015 this had been reduced to 15 per cent of the Parliamentary Labour Party, which meant 35 MPs.

then against Blair in '94. I don't think I could have beaten Blair, because at the time the Labour Party membership had lost a lot of confidence and moved to the right. I got kicked off Labour's NEC in '89, Skinner in '91 and Benn in '92. And it wasn't just that the machine was getting rid of us, after three Thatcher victories the rank and file were starting to think differently.

Looking back, perhaps the time wasn't right for a left-wing government then – with the collapse of the Berlin Wall Thatcher and Reagan felt their victories were cemented. But now things seem to be changing with social movements building in Europe and the US, the rise of Syriza, Podemos, the SNP… Are we beginning to witness the collapse of neoliberalism?

It hasn't completely collapsed, it's still controlling the banks and all of that. But look at Bernie Sanders in America. All across the world ordinary people are realising that they've been screwed the last 30 years and that this neoliberal agenda doesn't work. But the establishment will go to great lengths to try and prevent Jeremy or Bernie winning.

How do you feel if I put it to you that for the first time in a generation – since Tony Benn failed to get the deputy leadership of the Labour Party – the time could be right for a left-wing leader in the UK, and it's not you.

I'm 70. So I'd be 75 at the next election, and 80 at the end of my first term.

We've had older prime ministers in the past haven't we?

Yes but not at a time when there was the relentless day to day pressure. Churchill could spend two or three weeks in hospital, and no one knew he was there. It's very different now. The pressure is unremitting. It's the way things are.

It's the timings. If I'd got involved in politics much earlier, like Jeremy, who joined the Labour Party when he was about 16, I might have got into Parliament a lot sooner, I might have been an alternative to Kinnock. The other factor is that when I could have run for Labour leader, it was the highpoint of the neoliberal shift to the right. There's also the problem that my voice is the most unattractive voice in public life.

Your chief of staff, Simon Fletcher, was Jeremy Corbyn's campaign manager and now his own chief of staff, and your closest adviser Neale Coleman is Jeremy's policy chief. Surely there's a big role for you here?

I'll do anything that Jeremy wants, but there is also the small fact that I'm now a house husband.[7] I have to get the kids off to school in the morning and be here when they get back. I'm not going to go back into Parliament because Emma would have to give up her job and she's just spent four years getting her degree and becoming a teacher.

Also, until Jeremy actually wins the general election, there isn't much for him to hand out to do. I'm on Labour's NEC and I'll be supporting him and his programme going forward.

I'd like to end by talking about the health of democracy in the UK. You have talked about becoming mayor and the change you found in the media compared to the GLC and how pared down the media has now become.

This is the thing – 40 years ago there were twice the number of reporters in Britain than we've got today. I remember going into private radio stations and there'd be this huge room full of people all working there. You go in now and there's just 2 or

3 people producing each programme. Jobs have been scaled down everywhere they can possibly get away with it.

If I think back to when the Labour Party smeared me as a tax dodger in 2000, it was on the front page of the *Times* and there was a double-page spread inside saying I might be going to prison because of it. But the *Evening Standard*'s political correspondent checked the story out with the accountants and four hours later the *Standard*'s out saying 'it's complete rubbish'.

But when it came to the smears that I was a tax dodger in the 2012 election – not a single journalist phoned my accountant to ask anything. What you get now is that a smear appears, other papers repeat it and it's repeated on radio and television. No one checks anything. It's appalling.

A collapse in journalistic scrutiny is very serious for a functioning democracy, isn't it?

Our democracy's always been distorted by the fact that the public's been deceived on a massive scale, for example about the origins of the Cold War. Kennedy's is the first presidential election I remember, and it was all about the arms race and the Soviet Union. Now we know that his first briefing from the Pentagon was that they had 400 missiles capable of reaching Russia and they had four capable of reaching the USA. Russia didn't catch up until the mid '70s, and yet vast amounts of money were poured into armaments in the West and we were all told the Russians are ahead and all that. The same thing has been going on about the neoliberal agenda. We are all told Thatcher and Reagan saved us and that the 1970s were a disaster. What was wrong with the '70s was that the Saudi's quadrupled the price of oil in 1973 and that wrecked a lot of our manufacturing and fuelled inflation. Growth in the 30 years before Thatcher and Reagan in Britain and America was higher than it has been since.

But in the '80s, while there was warfare on the left and warfare between the Labour Party and the Conservative Party, there was a much higher standard of journalism, wasn't there?

Oh yes. Until Murdoch took over I used to read the *Times* because it was a paper of record. You might not agree with the editorial columns but it was a really good fact-based paper. Now there's the *Guardian* and the *Independent*, you wouldn't bother to read the *Times*. What's annoying is you expect this of the papers controlled by the tax-dodging billionaires, like Murdoch and the Barclay brothers and Rothermere. But the BBC isn't anything like as good as it should be in terms of actually explaining what's happening.

It holds back the left. How can the left mobilise public support when the public are just being told lies all the time by the media.

In 1987 you wrote that 'we must entwine democracy and socialism so they become inseparable'. You go on to say: 'In doing this we will change the nature and potential of both in ways we can only just begin to glimpse. Once such a process starts, it will be irreversible. Without such a process I doubt it will be possible for humankind to survive on this planet for much more than another lifetime.'[8] We've talked about New and old Labour failures in democracy, and of course it's hardly limited to Labour – it was the Tories who abolished the GLC and the Metropolitan Councils and emasculated local government – so it seems fair to say that there have been very major failures in democracy, a culture of corruption even, which has been prevalent for the last 35 years, probably longer. Is it now time for a fundamentally different culture of politics?

Yes. I would have a situation where you'd devolve virtually everything you can from Parliament and Westminster down to regions and local councils, so that people can influence things more locally. People have no influence over anything. If a local council is overseeing and managing their local NHS hospital, that can immediately open that up to accountability and openness. I'd do that with everything. I'd reduce central government to economic policy and foreign affairs and defence and that's about it. Central government can set national minimum standards, such as hospital waiting times, educational achievement, things like that, but not actually run these services.

Every health secretary, Labour and Tory, has failed to get a grip on the NHS. It must be one of the biggest employers in the world. It is too huge to be run from Whitehall. In Germany, about 50 per cent of state spending is by central government. Here it must be over 90 per cent. I'd just devolve everything you can.

Do you sympathise with the movement for independence in Scotland?

Well, no. The only difference independence would make, as opposed to proper devolution, would be that they could have their own armed forces and invade somewhere, and I don't see any point in that. Everything else can be devolved down. Same for Wales and all the English regions. And then you'd have a much smaller Westminster Parliament.

Do you think we should be trying to work towards a kinder culture in politics where the sort of ruthlessness of the political fix is seen as unacceptable?

It would be nice, but what you're talking about is a fairer redistribution of wealth. And the people who control all the wealth at the moment are not going to benignly agree to that. It's going to be vile. What they're going to throw at Jeremy

Corbyn is going to be worse than what they threw at me. It's not right and if Jeremy comes to power perhaps he can begin to change that. We're stuck with the current system until you get a Labour government that's going to be a genuine one.

What is interesting is that Jeremy does have an unblemished record of 30 years of public service as an MP, but this is seen as somehow exceptional, when in fact it's how everyone should behave. But he didn't want this job. He's got this job. Perhaps that's the best way of going about it. Not having spent your entire career as a Special Adviser and aiming to be a leading politician. I think that you and Jeremy Corbyn chose to be in public life as public servants because you're very interested in politics. But actually that seems quite different from a lot of career MPs, or is that unfair on a lot of them?

If you go back and read the things that Labour MPs wrote in the '50s and '60s, they were interested in politics too.

Well what happened to this generation?

This generation grew up getting more and more. And valuing wealth and expensive homes more and more, rather than public service. And so many Labour ministers were in awe of the financial sector and couldn't believe how people could make so much money.

Your career is obviously not over. It's got another act to go, at least. But I still want to end by asking you about Enoch Powell's famous dictum that 'all political careers end in failure'. How would you judge your own?

Well mine's a failure because I didn't get to be prime minister and I didn't create a social democratic heaven. I did some good things but I had the misfortune that just at the point when I was getting on to the national stage, there was this huge shift to the neoliberal right.

Thank you.

Additional material provided by Angharad Penrhyn Jones

CHAPTER THREE

Boris Will Be the Death of Me

by Ken Livingstone

You might find this hard to believe but it wouldn't have been possible to write this account of the 2012 mayoral election without the help of Alex Crowley, Political Director of Boris Johnson's campaign. Normally anything written by a candidate about their campaign is one-sided, self-obsessed and not worth reading. But Crowley's *Victory in London* is an honest insider account that allows me to take an overview of both campaigns rather than just defend my own.[1]

In the weekend following my 2008 defeat by Boris Johnson my closest friends and advisers urged me to say I would take Boris on again in 2012. But I was struggling to come to terms with my first election defeat since the general election in 1979 and I hadn't ruled out standing for Parliament so I wanted to put off the decision.

No one thought Gordon Brown would win the next election. Labour's vote had collapsed to just 24 per cent, our party was saddled with a £30 million debt from the 2005 general election, and half the cabinet were talking about a coup to replace Brown with David Miliband.

I wanted to be part of rebuilding a real Labour Party. But my friends thought I could do more for Londoners and Labour from City Hall. So with reluctance I announced I would be standing and set up a cross-party group called Progressive London to fight the carnage being wreaked by Boris.

At our first meeting 700 people turned up including Lib Dems, Greens and people of no affiliation to discuss how to tackle London's housing, transport and unemployment problems. As well as campaigning I wrote my autobiography and visited cities around the world whose mayors wanted advice on transport, the environment or how to win a bid for the Olympics.

Any doubts about challenging Boris were swept away as I watched his administration implode. Boris had not expected to win so there had been no planning for the transition. He had to spend £465,000 of City Hall funds to pay 15 'consultants' from Tory Central Office to oversee the transition.

Boris's key appointment to run City Hall was Tim Parker, who had amassed £75 million downsizing jobs at Clarks Shoes, KwikFit and the AA. After a few weeks he was forced out by Westminster councillor Simon Milton, another Boris adviser, who said he would quit if Parker stayed. Bexley Council Tory leader Ian Clement was made a deputy mayor but later sacked and prosecuted for credit card fraud. More embarrassing was Ray Lewis, who was in charge of tackling youth crime. After allegations of financial misconduct Boris defended Lewis but was gobsmacked when journalists raised sexual allegations and pointed out that Ray was not the magistrate he claimed to be. Not surprisingly Boris's key adviser Nick Boles quietly slipped away to pursue a parliamentary seat. Bob Diamond from Barclays Bank had agreed to run charity fundraising but also left after a few weeks. Boris's chief political adviser James McGrath was sacked for saying West Indians who didn't like Boris should leave the country.

Cameron was sucked in when Boris's Olympic adviser, David Ross (87th richest Brit and co-founder of Carphone Warehouse), used £162 million of shares to get a loan from JP Morgan without complying with the law. Boris said his actions were merely 'an oversight', but as the press exposed Ross's donations to the Tory Party, Boris 'accepted with regret' that he had to go. After paying off the incumbent, Boris brought in a new chief executive from Barnet Council but two years later paid him a quarter of a million pounds to leave. Boris kept his adviser Anthony Browne even after it came out that he feared immigrants would bring diseases that would wipe out all Brits.

The press paid less attention to the huge cuts Boris made. Although I left a surplus of £1.5 billion (out of a £12 billion budget) Boris increased bus fares by a third and cut police numbers by 455. Altogether £2.4 billion was cut from transport and £3.5 billion of investment in tram and DLR extensions was cancelled. The plan to build a bridge across the Thames at Newham was dropped, and a scheme to improve Oxford Street by replacing polluting buses with a tram service also bit the dust. Although I had persuaded Gordon Brown to give us £5 billion to build 50,000 affordable homes in three years, Boris never achieved this and also abolished my rule that half of all new homes built should be affordable.

The only inherited project Boris did not scrap was the cycle hire scheme, but it was restricted to the city centre and worked out at £12,000 for each bike and docking frame. The majority of users were earning over £50,000 a year. Our offices in China and India, which brought jobs to London, were closed, even though we had got £21 million of investment from China in just 12 months.

Plans to improve air quality were dumped when Boris dropped proposals for a charge on polluting 4x4s. This meant he had to pay Porsche £430,000 towards their legal costs as they had gone to court to try and stop it. He also postponed the next stage of the Low Emission Zone.

Gordon Brown didn't want me standing again. His spin doctor Damien McBride wrote 'we needed a realistic alternative to block Ken Livingstone from standing again ... I hinted to one newspaper we were looking at Alan Sugar [but]

I got an urgent message that [Sugar] was furious and wanted the story killed.'[2] When the banks crashed Brown stopped worrying about who was going to be the next mayor.

Just before the general election, Ray Collins, the general secretary of the Labour Party, gave me a lift home after a fundraiser where we were both speaking. I had a lot of sympathy for Ray. He had been parachuted into the post of general secretary after the unexplained departure of his predecessor. He inherited vast debts, a demoralised party and Labour running under 30 per cent in the polls.

We quickly struck up a rapport and he asked if I was serious about standing and got my view about when Labour should select its candidate. I was certain we needed a candidate who could rebuild the party machine. I was doing meetings in key marginal seats all over London and had been stunned at the decimation of Labour's machine.

Anger over the war in Iraq and New Labour's failure to tackle inequality meant that 60 per cent of members had resigned or allowed their membership to lapse. In 2000 we had 80,000 members in London, now it was just 30,000, and in some areas the Labour machine had virtually ceased to exist.

Ray had a more mundane reason for preferring an early selection. Labour was £26 million in debt and technically bankrupt. He wanted to save on postage by using the same envelopes for members to cast their ballots for the next Labour leader and mayoral candidate. Some Blairites complained this was a stitch up and we should put the selection off until after the election of our next leader.

Simon Fletcher, my chief of staff from City Hall, lined up a campaign team in case another candidate came forward. Some Blairites wanted Alan Johnson or Peter Mandelson, but the only person who expressed an interest was Oona King. In her autobiography she wrote that she would love to be mayor, but at a charity fundraiser, while walking over 20 feet of burning coals together, she hadn't said she was going to stand so I was a bit surprised when she decided to. Perhaps she was just concentrating on not getting her feet burnt!

Although demonised as a New Labour clone I liked Oona and got on with her. Like me she had two young children and we were able to swap tales of the pleasures and horrors of parenthood. She had urged me to stand as an independent in the 2000 mayoral election. Along with dozens of other MPs she was pressured by Alastair Campbell to denounce me but she refused.

In the 2005 general election I worked to help Oona although she had supported the invasion of Iraq. She recognised that was a mistake and I didn't think that one error should obliterate her very good record in representing her constituents.

Oona did decide to stand and many of her activists came from Progress, the Blairite group funded by Lord Sainsbury (a quarter of a million pounds a year) and the British Venture Capital Association, which promotes privatisation. The contest became more of a referendum on New Labour than about London's needs. Her campaign team refused to oppose the Royal Mail sell off and their emphasis on my age chimed perfectly with attacks from Boris's team.

I launched my campaign with a walkabout in Croydon in the first week of June, promising to reinstate plans to extend the tram that had been cancelled by Boris. It took an hour to make the short walk from George Street to North End. The rain did not stop hundreds of shoppers clamouring around for selfies and handshakes and even the *Croydon Advertiser* (not my natural supporter) pointed out 'He may not be New Labour's favourite son … but the charisma is still there and judging by the public's response on Tuesday many … think he's still the best choice to wrestle back the mayoralty from that other larger than life character Boris Johnson.'

The *Evening Standard* revealed I was now a grandfather following the birth of baby Sky, pointing out I would be 67 the following week and almost 71 by the end of the next mayoral term. They dug up Labour MP Nick Raynsford who warned that I was almost as old as he was and it was 'time for someone new', so we changed our slogan 'Yes We Ken' to 'Yes We Ken Be a Grandfather and Mayor'.

The first debate with Oona was in Ilford North where over 50 members turned up for what the *Guardian*'s Dave Hill described as an 'assiduously cordial' meeting. Oona described me as 'one of her heroes' and argued that white working-class families in outer London felt the Labour Party didn't really care about them or what happens to their kids or their future and she would want to reverse that. This chimed so perfectly with my view of Labour's failures that I immediately decided that if I became mayor I would put Oona in charge of childcare and education.

Oona's friendly approach wasn't shared by her campaign team. Their leaflets recycled the *Evening Standard* smears from the 2008 campaign claiming that for over 'a decade London's City Hall has been dogged with … allegations of cronyism'. They claimed that both I and Boris had a 'no can do approach' and that 'during the eight years of Ken's mayoralty allegations … eroded public trust'.

A Twitterer called No2Ken took up the age issue with comments like 'let's stop 65 year old Ken Livingstone from being Labour's mayoral candidate' and 'Ken does not relate to Londoners, we need a young fresh and energetic hopeful for Labour. We need to wake up and smell the coffee. We need to put up a fresh new opponent against Boris. I cannot believe Labour is serious about anti-Semitic Ken Livingstone as mayor of London.' Boriswatch didn't take long to discover that the tweeter was Einy Shah, an ex-Boris aide whose website even attracted support from Tea Party activists in the USA.

Oona was rubbished by the *Jewish Chronicle* because on a trip to Gaza she had likened the conditions there to those in the Warsaw ghetto. The *Chronicle*'s Marcus Dysch dismissed her bid for support 'because her previous stance on the Israeli-Palestinian conflict angered the Jewish community … And Boris, the love bomber, remains the community's clear favourite to continue as mayor of London.'[3]

As our campaign was running alongside the Labour leadership contest we were always being asked who we supported. Knowing Oona's politics I wasn't surprised when she came out for Ed rather than David Miliband. She said that her commitment to Ed dated back to 2006 when she heard him making a speech which lifted the room 'in a way that I did not know you could do – it took my breath away'. Oona was one of the first to urge Ed to run once Gordon Brown resigned.

I used my second preference for Ed Miliband but I campaigned for Ed Balls. Although we had political differences I was impressed by Balls' ability when negotiating with him to get support for big London projects. I spent more time in meetings with government ministers than anything else. Some were abysmal non-entities who merely read out the brief their civil servants had written for them. But when I met Ed Balls it was on a one-to-one basis and he would make a decision. The most impressive was in 2007 when over dinner he agreed to find £5 billion to build Crossrail, which had been on hold for 40 years and will finally open in 2018. The next day my finance director queried the bill as it included two bottles of wine, but stopped complaining when I pointed out it had taken four hours and we were getting £5 billion in return.

After I lost the mayoralty Ed Balls and I discussed who would succeed Brown. David Miliband had galvanised the Blairite wing and the only other name in the frame was Balls himself. Ed Miliband had not made up his mind at this point. Although I had expected David to succeed Brown we fell out when he sided with his officials to block my plans to recycle waste rather than incinerating it. I believed Labour needed a leader who stood up to civil servants so I urged Balls to stand against David.

Housing had become London's biggest problem since Mrs Thatcher stopped council house building in 1979. Post-war Britain built 400,000 houses a year, half private and half council houses for rent, but that collapsed by half as Blair continued Thatcher's ban. Contrary to Tory predictions, the private sector never filled the gap created by Thatcher. Ed Balls recognised this was one of Labour's failings and committed to a major house building programme which would create three quarters of a million new jobs as well as tackling ridiculous rents and house prices.

No one was certain of the outcome of the selection process, but under the headline 'The Undead Red' the *Economist* warned of 'Ken Livingstone's latest comeback':

> Mr Livingstone has a gift for campaigning and a mastery of machine politics that his rival lacks … [He] has secured the nominations of major trade unions … and the backing of most of the Labour members of the London Assembly. There are whispers that Mr Johnson may not run again and while he has lots of small accomplishments to his name … he cannot point to a defining triumph such as the congestion charge Mr Livingstone introduced in 2003.[4]

Just days before the result I was plunged into despair. Once again it was the poisonous politics of Tower Hamlets Labour Party. Throughout the 1970s our councillors had become more representative of the London demographic – except in Tower Hamlets where it took until 1982 for an Asian councillor to be elected. At the GLC we funded desperately poor Bangladeshi community groups and I urged them to join the party. In 1986 lots of candidates of Bangladeshi origin were selected but the old leadership stood as independents to split the Labour vote, which allowed the Liberals to win. For eight years they embarrassed the Liberals nationally by pandering to racism and excluding the Bangladeshi community.

Labour won in 1994 under the leadership of John Biggs, an honest and competent leader who was soon overthrown by a clique who played divide and rule tactics in the community. Local councillor Kumar Murshid, one of my mayoral advisers, joked that Bangladeshis were only allowed positions once they had been 'house trained'. As he prepared to stand for Labour leader in Tower Hamlets Kumar was framed on a corruption charge by the new leadership clique and suspended from the Labour Party. With the help of his lawyer Sadiq Khan (now candidate for the 2016 mayoral election) he was cleared, but he was off the council because Labour had barred him from standing. It was not until 2008 that Lutfur Rahman broke the hold of the clique and became Labour leader, implementing a progressive agenda that ensured Tower Hamlets became the first borough to pay staff a living wage, a policy I had started four years earlier.

Because of the infighting, Labour Party membership in Tower Hamlets was managed by the regional Labour office to prevent any dodgy practices. When the borough voted in a referendum to have a directly elected mayor Lutfur Rahman won the ballot to be Labour's candidate but the old guard sent a report to Labour's NEC implying he had links to terrorists. NEC members only saw the report when they arrived at the meeting just a couple of days before the close of nominations for the Tower Hamlets mayoral election. There was no time to summon Lutfur to answer these charges so the NEC was bounced into imposing an old guard councillor in his place.

I was devastated. One of the things that makes me proud to be British is that British people have the right to defend themselves from allegations and not be found guilty in secret hearings from which the public are excluded. Shamefully the NEC ignored this principle and believed the campaign directed at Lutfur by the journalist Andrew Gilligan. One NEC member even said 'this has been in the newspapers so there must be some truth in it'. I was in despair. I could not believe my party had done this. If, on top of this, David had become leader while still refusing to admit the Iraq War was wrong, I would have quit as Labour's candidate.

After the result was announced, Oona and I remained friends and I helped at her fundraiser to pay off her campaign debts. Boris's deputy, Kit Malthouse, said Labour had 'exhumed a game old boy', and the *Evening Standard* did its bit by putting my age in brackets every time they mentioned me.

The next day at Labour's conference I watched Ed and David Miliband embrace as it was announced that Ed had won. Neil Kinnock almost hugged me as he joyfully exclaimed 'We've got our party back again!' Although I had used my second preference vote for Ed I had not dealt with him while I was mayor. We had exchanged pleasantries as we passed in corridors but he never had ministerial responsibilities covering London until after I lost the election. I knew he wasn't New Labour and had opposed another runway at Heathrow. I was impressed when the expenses scandal erupted and he was 567th down the list claiming only £7,670, in contrast to Osborne, Nick Clegg and Boris who maxed out their parliamentary expenses by getting mortgages big enough to claim the maximum possible of £23,000 a year (with Cameron a close runner up on £19,626).

That evening Ed said a few words alongside me at the London Labour Party reception and I steered him away from being photographed with Labour's candidate for Tower Hamlets, quietly warning him to have nothing to do with him. The following week we met in his office and although I thought he seemed very young to be party leader I warmed to his openness and good humour. He saw my election as a trial run for the general election and brought in Patrick Heneghan to run my campaign with Simon.

At the Tory conference delegates laughed as Boris said 'The Labour Party has responded to the challenge of finding a new mayoral candidate with stupefying lack of originality. They have found a piece of DNA preserved in the tar pits of Cricklewood. Like Holmes and Moriarty, like Harry Potter and Voldemort, this contest is fated to continue for more than one episode.' But a YouGov poll on 10th October showed Boris was only ahead by 46 to 44 per cent. I led in every age group except the over 55s and was 2 per cent ahead of the Labour Party nationally. Londoners felt I had done a good job as mayor by 56 per cent to 36, I was seen as more competent than Boris by 52 to 45 and more in touch with Londoners than he was by 44 to 40.

In his book, Alex Crowley says that Boris's team had their first meeting to discuss the 2012 campaign as early as the end of 2008. City Hall's polls showed the number of Londoners saying they knew what the mayor's responsibilities were was just 39 per cent, compared with 51 per cent in my last year, and those saying they had no opinion on how the mayor was doing had gone up from 17 per cent to 32 per cent. Crowley concluded that Boris would remain popular 'even in the teeth of a recession and a plunging Tory poll rating ... but his achievements did not spring readily to voters' minds'.[5]

Worried that Labour had won 2 per cent more votes than the Tories in London in the 2010 general election, Boris appointed Lynton Crosby, the most effective propagandist since Dr Joseph Goebbels (only joking). Crosby believed 'You can't fatten the pig on market day', and true to his word had Boris's re-election campaign in place even before I won the Labour nomination. The *Evening Standard*'s deputy news editor Sam Lyon was also recruited and by September 2010 Boris's campaign office had opened, opinion polling was underway and the website about to launch.

Crosby's control of the campaign was total. After a debate in which Boris deviated from the line by claiming 'fares will go down in an honest and sustainable way under me', Crosby berated him in front of everybody, including my staff, telling him 'if you let us down we will cut your fucking knees off'. The *Mail on Sunday* reported he told Boris to 'concentrate on traditional Tory voters instead of fucking Muslims'.[6] Crosby told Boris: 'imagine you are in trouble. The facts are overwhelmingly against you, the more people focus on reality the worse it is for you. Your best bet in these circumstances is to throw a dead cat on the table mate. Everyone will shout jeez mate there's a dead cat on the table, they will be talking about the dead cat and not the issue that's been causing you so much grief.'

Although he denied it, the Australian Anonymous Lefty website alleged that Crosby said 'It's just a job which I happen to be very good at, but in the dead of night the fact that my campaign strategy so often boils down to dishonesty haunts me. I hope my kids never realise.'

Crosby decided the theme should be 'not Ken again', to focus on the 17 per cent of Labour voters who said they would rather have Boris as mayor than me. According to Crowley, Crosby was 'carefully preparing the ground behind the scenes, raising money, building an organisation and doing the extensive homework on Ken Livingstone that would prove so lethal during the election. They were determined that this campaign would be much better prepared, organised and effective than Ken's.'

Crowley also reveals they had 'regular and numerous leaks' from my campaign, including 'large sections of Ken's "warbook" … key elements of strategy, major announcements and how many supporters [we] had in certain areas'.[7] We did not know it at the time but it seems fairly certain a Labour Party agent was passing information to Boris's office, although this was never proved. What shocked me was that this individual was really friendly, completely supportive and often picked me up from home to drive me to meetings. I don't know if they did it for money or because they were angered by the selection of Ed Miliband and myself.

Over the next year I spent a day in each of London's 32 boroughs. The need to rebuild Labour's machine was starkest in the Tory suburbs. In Orpington, I was moved by the warm reception I received from people who were struggling desperately to make ends meet. One told me he hadn't seen anyone from the Labour Party in Orpington since the by-election. As the by-election had been in 1962 we had a lot of work to do. In two weeks we made more contacts in Bromley than in the previous 15 years. It was the same in Carshalton, where activists said they had been ignored and never had help during the years of New Labour.

The visits really boosted our confidence and Val Shawcross, the London Assembly Member I had chosen to be my deputy mayor, loved chairing the public question and answer sessions that we had at the end of each visit. At every meeting there were always Tories present, recording everything I said.

Work began on drawing up policies to rebalance London's economy. Boris had cancelled all the tram and light rail schemes I had been planning, so I committed to reinstate them. When we spent £1.4 billion upgrading and extending the North London line usage more than doubled. The Labour government had amended the GLA act to put two people on the Transport for London (TfL) board to represent train commuters from outside London, and as each franchise came up for renewal it would come under the mayor's control. But Boris dropped the idea and London's suburban rail service was left to rot.

The £5 billion Brown had offered City Hall to build 50,000 affordable homes hadn't been spent and London's housing crisis worsened. The failure to build council housing meant the private rented sector had doubled in size with many dodgy landlords abusing their tenants, so we drew up plans for the mayor to crack down on bad landlords.

When I was mayor the government's scientific advisers estimated that 1,200 Londoners a year died prematurely because of poor air quality. To cut this pollution I introduced a Low Emission Zone, but Boris had deferred the next stage and halved the size of the congestion zone (which had cut pollution by 15 per cent). In 2010 the scientists revised their estimate, warning that in fact 4,300 people died prematurely each year (more than were killed on 9/11 and 20 times our annual road casualties).

This meant that one Londoner in twenty would die prematurely unless we reduced nitrous oxides and particulates. Buses and taxis were two of the main polluters so I met with a manufacturer who had produced an electric bus (we could use the same technology on taxis). Alongside the phasing out of diesel cars and HGVs this could solve our problem. After 40 years working in the heart of polluted London my lung capacity is as bad as a man five years older, so as one of the 400,000 Londoners facing premature death I had a motive for removing Boris. Throughout the campaign Boris denied our air quality was so bad. But I was amazed when on a visit to Japan to discuss the Olympic legacy I found it easier to breath in the centre of Tokyo than I do in London.

The mood in Labour's HQ was electric, with activists manning phone banks, working on research and organising canvassing teams across London. The polls were still close. YouGov put me two points ahead of Boris in February. City Hall's own poll showed a big drop in the number of Londoners saying they had seen police on the streets, and a big rise in the number worried by the cost of fares. Those saying they knew what the mayor was doing were 9 per cent down. Those satisfied with the way Boris was doing his job were just 32 per cent (my final rating was 44 per cent).

Our secret weapon turned out to be Coco, our yellow Labrador puppy. Tom and Mia had wanted a dog for years and we bought them off with a succession of snakes, lizards and a hamster, but as Emma and I were now working from home there was no reason not to get a puppy. I hadn't had a dog since I left home and had forgotten how much they are a complete part of the family. Coco was the best behaved dog I have ever known and everyone on the campaign team fell in love with her as she joined us on walkabouts. Photographers asked me to bring her with me saying it was the only way they could guarantee to get my picture in the paper, and I spent many interviews with Coco lying patiently at my feet. Coco also reconnected me with nature. On our daily dog walks in my local park I saw the slow change of the seasons and realised how the daily grind of rushing from home to office, commuting through tunnels and on roads cuts us off from nature.

Emma and I were making final corrections to my autobiography when police shot Mark Duggan dead in Tottenham in August 2011. There was no response from the mayor's office or his deputy mayor for policing. When police mistakenly shot Jean Charles de Menezes after the London tube bombings we dispatched Assistant Commissioner Yates to Brazil to personally apologise to his family, and Commissioner Ian Blair and myself immediately went on television to apologise. Two days after Duggan's shooting his family led a protest to Tottenham police station to demand answers to why Mark had been killed. No one was there to meet them and they left after several hours. Anger exploded triggering riots across London. Boris was on holiday and his political advisers were at a wedding in Spain. As news of the riots broke they carried on with the party, announcing the next day that Boris would not 'reward' the rioters by returning to London. I was gobsmacked remembering how I felt in Singapore when the 7/7 bombs went off and I just wanted to be back home doing whatever I could. Days went by, the riots worsened, much of Croydon was on fire, and public outrage forced Boris to return. Ed Miliband and I had already been out seeing the consequences of the riots and Ed held a meeting of council leaders where we discussed what could be done. When Boris did finally appear he received a hostile reaction. 'Why are you here now?' and 'three days too late' yelled the crowd. Home Secretary Theresa May sensibly slipped away. Eventually Boris dissipated some of the anger by grabbing a broom and urging people to start clearing up the mess.

Boris's team were worried. Crowley writes: 'it was obvious that many of Boris's own team, like the public, could not recall what had been achieved'. Their polling showed it was neck and neck and that we were the only two politicians in London with a positive rating. Boris's team feared I could win because of my 'relentless focus on the bread and butter issues'.

Crosby dispatched a team to the British Library's press archive to pour over every story that had appeared during my eight years as mayor. Every item of expenditure during my mayoralty was checked out in detail. Having been told to get in shape, Boris hired Baby Spice's personal trainer.

Tory worries increased when at Labour's conference in 2011 I promised to cut bus and tube fares by 5 per cent. Boris was increasing fares by 2 per cent above inflation every year creating a £700 million surplus which could not be justified whilst Londoners struggled to make ends meet. Crowley writes: 'the election was in danger of becoming a referendum on fares which the research showed Boris would lose every time.'[8] Tory polling showed 59 per cent of Londoners wanted fares kept down. To cut the surplus the Tories ordered TfL to repay £277 million of debts early.

However, Labour's private polling was causing even more despair in our campaign. A ComRes poll in June gave Boris a 6 per cent lead. We hoped that this might be a freak result but we were wrong. For three years Boris had depoliticised the office of mayor. His press office generated endless feel-good photo ops with the mayor on his bike, at charity events, society parties and opening the projects I had initiated. Journalists were not allowed serious interviews and only six press conferences had been held in three years. When fare increases or cuts in policing happened Boris wasn't available for interview. This strategy worked, with polls showing many Londoners didn't think it mattered who was mayor because it wasn't a very political role.

We had commissioned a poll of 2,000 Londoners and it was shattering. Boris had a 29 per cent lead over me on the issue of charisma although I had a 14 per cent lead on who was most in touch with Londoners and on fares policy. The pollsters identified 6 per cent of London voters who were inclined towards Labour but preferred Boris to me.

The big concerns of that 6 per cent were crime, immigration and tougher sentencing. What was most annoying was the majority of the 6 per cent thought it was Boris who had brought the Olympics to London and introduced neighbourhood police patrols. They also believed Boris was more in touch with Londoners and more likely to cut fares. Amongst Londoners as a whole there were 2 per cent who thought I was 'an old fashioned lefty', but amongst this key 6 per cent that rose to 38 per cent. That 6 per cent were 50 per cent more likely to be readers of the *Evening Standard*. The only encouraging point was that when asked at the beginning of the survey who they would vote for, Boris had an 18 per cent lead, but after being shown our policies the gap narrowed to just six points (although two thirds of the 6 per cent still intended to vote for Boris). The pollsters' conclusion was that 'this is tough but there is movement possible', and we needed to show that 'Ken is on the side of ordinary Londoners and Boris is not.'

I so wanted to be mayor again as there was so much I wanted to do for Londoners, but I decided that if anyone else had a better chance of defeating Boris I would stand aside. I put this to Labour's national agent Hillary Perrin who exploded. She gave me a short, sharp lecture on why there wasn't anyone else who could do any better and I couldn't walk away from this contest. We couldn't beat Boris on campaign expenditure or get fair coverage in the Tory papers so we had to build a machine to get the vote out.

Given the poor polls many people advised Ed Miliband to avoid my campaign and it says a lot for him that he ignored that advice. I was impressed how quickly Ed grew into his job over those two years. In our meetings he focused on what we would do for London and Britain rather than be obsessed with the media or how he appeared. After years of politicians pandering to vested interests it was a relief to watch a Labour leader stand up to Murdoch and the banks and tell energy and rail companies that their prices were too high. He didn't just admit that the war in Iraq was wrong, he also apologised for Brown's mistakes. He did not come into politics to be loved but because he wanted a fairer Britain. Not since the death of John Smith have I seen a party leader with the strength of character to do precisely that.

On 28th November, the day after the *Evening Standard*'s headline 'Four more years of Boris says poll' (with Boris at 54 per cent), George Osborne did his bit to help by announcing that he would give extra money to reduce fare increases allowing Boris to cut the increase to just 1 per cent above inflation. My team immediately reworked the figures and discovered TfL's surplus was even bigger, allowing us to cut fares not just by 5 per cent but by 7 per cent, saving the average fare-payer £250 a year.

As I announced the 7 per cent cut on 5th December, Lynton Crosby turned to Crowley saying 'Mate, he's back in the game.' Crowley continues: 'The Labour machine was very impressive. The sheer ruthlessness with which they hammered home the message about fares … was causing our campaign some concern. Every time Ken or any Labour politician appeared … on any issue all they would talk about was fares.'[9] Boris's response was to tell the *Evening Standard* he would introduce driverless tube trains on the Victoria, Central, Jubilee and Northern Lines within two years. Four years on, still waiting!

By 19th January a YouGov poll put me ahead of Boris by 51 to 49 per cent. It showed that only 13 per cent thought Boris was in touch with ordinary Londoners compared with my 40 per cent. Patrick, Simon and the team were elated but I said I would rather I was still behind as this was bound to unleash a very dirty Tory response. We had a sign of what was to come when City Hall said my fares pledge showed I was a schizophrenic.

We were also campaigning against Boris's cut in the number of police officers, which he denied. Finally LBC's Nick Ferrari pinned him down saying 'You're down 1,700 in the last two years.' Boris waffled, 'numbers go up and down, they naturally fluctuate'. 'By 1,700?' said Ferrari. 'Yes, but…' replied Boris. Crowley reports Crosby started screaming abuse as he listened to the interview.

On 7th February Crowley watched a focus group of Bromley voters being questioned. They had all voted for Boris in 2008 but were now undecided, believing Boris was more concerned about his prime ministerial ambitions than Londoners. They thought I was more likely to help them as they struggled to make ends meet. The only thing they knew Boris had done was the bike hire scheme. Crosby's business partner Mark Textor said, 'in 20 years of polling, this was the clearest example of a group of voters being one step away from saying "fuck it, you're not worth it". It was a crisis point', and City Hall should 'stop the banal, celebrity crap at once'. Crosby's response was to accelerate 'our plans for a negative campaign against Livingstone'.[10] A thousand poster sites were rented with negative 'Not Ken Again' posters warning I would increase council tax, break my promises and rely on Bob Crow. 'Bob Crow was to feature heavily in all our anti-Ken material',[11] says Crowley, who spent long nights going over every City Hall grant and my personal credit card statements.

The Tories also checked out those close to me, including the mother of my eldest boy Liam, who was born in 1992. They discovered she had been supporting (but was not paid by) Rootball Productions when they produced a play about slavery which was funded by City Hall. She had also worked at Stockwell Park Community Trust while the trust applied for a planning permission that I agreed. This information was passed to Tory MP Priti Patel who demanded an enquiry which was dragged out until after the election, when the smears were all dismissed by City Hall's independent monitoring officer.

Boris could no longer avoid debates and on 21st February we all turned up at the Age UK hustings. I produced a large pledge card saying that if elected I would do only the mayor's job, pointing out that Boris had earned £1 million, which he dismissed as 'chicken feed', writing a weekly *Daily Telegraph* column. I said 'If you can't live on a mayor's salary of £140,000 you must have a very interesting lifestyle.' Boris's speech was a rerun of his campaign speech four years earlier, and as we left the crowded hall everyone agreed not just that I had beaten Boris but so had the Lib Dem candidate Brian Paddick.

The dirty or 'dead cat' campaign I had feared arrived on 26th February. Like the smears in the 2008 election it was begun by Andrew Gilligan. He claimed in the *Telegraph* that I had set up a company to avoid paying tax. My earnings after I lost the 2008 election – with the exception of my weekly radio programme on LBC – were all on a one-off basis, giving after dinner speeches or advice to overseas cities, and I would have been mad not to have an accountant and a company to manage my income. The Tories claimed I only had to pay corporation tax at 20 per cent rather than income tax at 40 per cent, but a small company pays 20 per cent corporation tax as the money comes in, and then you pay another 20 per cent personal income tax when you take out a salary, so paying 40 per cent in total.

A lot of my work was unpaid for charities or the Labour Party, so travel and accommodation costs came out of the company. Emma, who had managed my office as mayor and been forced to leave by Boris, now ran the company, helped me write my autobiography, and managed my visits, diary and travel arrangements. We both paid tax on our earnings, full national insurance, and I did not claim my state pension. Over three years the company amassed £140,000 profit so I used £70,000 of that to pay for a researcher and a press officer to work on the campaign. This was declared as a donation to the Labour Party from my company.

Hundreds of thousands of small firms operate in the same way. Tax cheats launder their money through offshore companies or investment scams like funding films that never get made. When Gilligan phoned I told him this was how his bosses, the Barclay Brothers, did their tax scams, but he left that out of the article. The only advantage of owning a small company is that the income from one year can be spread over future years if your income declines – as mine certainly did in the run up to the election.

Just how relentlessly the Tories pushed the issue was revealed at Prime Minister's Questions as Tory backbenchers got Cameron to accuse me of tax avoidance. Sadly it was only after the election that the *Guardian* discovered that Cameron's family fortune was amassed by his father's laundering money offshore. Angry old Blairites like former candidate Jonathan Roberts and blogger Dan Hodges echoed the smear. Simon Jenkins wrote that any tax saving is more than cancelled by the accountants' fees. On the Andrew Marr show I revealed that Boris had the same tax arrangements, with his earnings from television going into his own company.

I came into politics to do things, not to get rich. As an MP I had no difficulty living on my parliamentary salary so all my extra earnings were paid into the company I used to employ staff for research, secretarial help and to pay £7,000 a year to hire what was then the largest computer not owned by government or big business. This analysed economic data to challenge Thatcher's policies and to produce the *Socialist Economic Bulletin* (still available online). As mayor my salary doubled and some said I should buy a more expensive house, but I never saw my home as an investment.

The next day the *Sun* had a photo of me bare-chested in my gardening gear putting out the rubbish. It was the only time in the campaign a hidden photographer watched my house and the only weekend during the campaign when Emma was away. Was my phone being hacked and the *Sun* hoping I'd be entertaining someone I shouldn't?

The dirty tricks continued as we launched the slogan 'Better off with Ken'. Crowley says this had been leaked to them so they pre-empted us with a 'Better off with Boris' launch. Boris claimed my fares cut would mean TfL would have to cut investment. The *Evening Standard* claimed Moody's ratings agency had produced a report saying TfL would collapse if I cut the fares. This was completely untrue as Moody's report showed TfL now had a £1 billion surplus with the income from fares 5.9 per cent more than expected, expenditure 8 per cent lower and investment 14.5 per cent lower than the previous year.

The smears were not confined to the media. A man in Croydon said he couldn't vote for me because the Tory who canvassed him said I would introduce Sharia law. Another voter in Newham told me he had been warned I planned to build a mega mosque if elected.

The first broadcast debate was at LBC on 3rd April, chaired by Nick Ferrari. After all the work investigating my City Hall finances, Crowley had only dug up that I twice made the mistake of using the City Hall credit card (to buy a cup of coffee and a shirt). The only other item was a pair of snow shoes I bought before I went to represent London at the World Economic Forum at Davos. It was cheaper to buy snow shoes and walk between events than hiring a car. For Boris's trips to Davos, City Hall shelled out a small fortune for his chauffeurs.

Boris erupted when I said his successful campaign to cut the top rate of tax meant he was paying £12,000 a year less, saying this was 'a reprehensible accusation'. But he got even angrier when I said we both had the same tax arrangements for dealing with our media earnings. Red in the face he shouted: 'That is a complete lie. The man's a liar.' I replied: 'Boris we both had media earnings, we both put them through a company.' 'No, that's not true. The guy's a liar, a barefaced liar.' After the debate we were all in the lift and I jokingly asked Brian Paddick 'isn't it time for a citizen's arrest?' Boris shouted 'You fucking liar' three times whilst staring at the floor. Brian, Jenny Jones and myself just smiled at each other. Crowley wasn't unhappy when the *Standard* and regional TV led with the story, as 'this was another day when the story was about Ken's tax arrangements … It wasn't about fares.'[12]

Just before the start of the next debate Boris came up to me and asked 'Are we alright?' When I said 'No, I'm not happy with the lies coming from your campaign', he looked hurt and shuffled off. On the *Newsnight* debate Jenny suggested we all publish our tax returns. I jumped at the idea and the next day people were able to see I had paid 34 per cent tax on my income and Boris who was earning more than twice as much paid 41 per cent as he was in the top tax bracket. After the election when we filed my tax returns in 2012 we discovered I had overpaid tax to the tune of £10,459.

The tax smear was dispiriting but my team were boosted by the candidates' debates. Even in the debate organised by City finance firms Boris struggled to achieve a score draw. Given that the majority of his campaign funding came from hedge fund donations this was amazing.

The most inspiring debate was with London's churches. There were murmurs of dissent when Brian referred to Islam as a peaceful religion, so I quoted the prophet Mohammed who, knowing he was dying, set out a creed for living in his last sermon. It was centuries ahead of its time. 'An Arab has no superiority over a non-Arab, nor a non-Arab any superiority over an Arab. Also a white has no superiority over a black nor a black any superiority over a white.' Mohammed then said God created humanity 'and formed you into tribes and nations so that you may get to know one another. Not so you may fight or oppress or occupy or convert or terrorise but so that you may get to know one another.' The audience's applause was louder than at any other time in the campaign.

It is quite clear that the monstrous tactics of Osama bin Laden and Isis with their beheadings and mass murders are completely at loggerheads with the teachings of Mohammed, but the more Western politicians and journalists depict these extremists as typical of Islam, the more they stir up Islamophobia with the danger of alienating good Muslims and driving them into the hands of extremists.

I repeated that same quote to similar applause when the issue of homophobia in the Muslim community came up at the lesbian and gay hustings. At all these debates Boris struggled as the audience brought up his reactionary writings and lack of action. He just waffled when reminded of his claim that if two men could 'tie the knot why not three men and a dog?'

I expected Boris to be well received at the hustings for cyclists but they had seen through his cosmetic policies. While he continued my bike hire scheme, the cycle routes I had planned were reduced to painting blue lanes along busy roads after Boris cancelled the other proposed safety measures. Tragically two cyclists had been killed at the Bow roundabout and local bike groups said the scheme's separation measures had been removed by the mayor's office. Boris bellowed that it wasn't true.

With the exception of the bankers' event, Boris had been the loser in all the debates because he lacked the detail that Jenny, Brian and myself were able to give. Things were no better for him in the television debates. His worst performance was with Andrew Neil, who kept up relentless pressure as Boris waffled on about whether he wanted to be prime minister. Andrew contemptuously turned his back on him saying 'We'll take that as a yes then.' Even on Murdoch's Sky debate, where the subject of fares was left until last, Boris still struggled, particularly as I produced a TfL report showing their budget surplus was still growing so making the fares cut easier.

Although some polls gave Boris a big lead, others still had it close enough that the BBC's *Question Time* debate could be the decisive factor. David Dimbleby had presided over a debate between Boris, Brian and myself four years earlier, with the best viewing figures of the season. The BBC agreed in January that the debate would be on the Thursday before polling day and would include Jenny as well as Brian. But a week before it was due to air the BBC cancelled the debate claiming it was only a local London issue and that *Question Time* was a national programme. Twitter reported that Dimbleby was furious.

When my press officer, Jo Derrett, lobbied hard for the BBC to reverse its decision, their reason for cancelling switched to the equally unconvincing claim that the independent candidate Siobhan Benita might go to court over not being included, even though she had not challenged her exclusion from any of the other debates and told me she didn't have the money to bring a legal challenge. I really regret not blowing this up as a huge issue but I had been campaigning for nearly two years and was absolutely exhausted with an unremitting schedule of visits and meetings. Foolishly I let it go.

After the election someone in Boris's team (not Crowley) told me they put daily pressure on the BBC over their coverage, including the demand to cancel the debate and to stop the candidates being interviewed on Radio 4's *Today* programme. The idea that in a six-week campaign *Today* couldn't find time to interview the four main party candidates was pathetic. John Humphreys had interviewed Oona and me two years earlier during Labour's mayoral selection.

Tories complain about left-wing bias at the BBC but I never noticed it. After I lost in 2008 the BBC's 'Who Do You Think You Are?' programme took details of my family history so they could do a programme to follow Boris's appearance on the same show. They came back to say they had been told to drop the idea because it wouldn't be right for the programme to appear before the 2012 election. As it was over three years away, this was rubbish. When I asked who had taken this decision I was told 'it came from the top'. The BBC also vetoed my making a cameo appearance on EastEnders, even though Boris was allowed to appear, and ignoring our protests they agreed to televise Boris presenting the winner of the Oxford and Cambridge boat race with the trophy, even though this was during the election campaign.

Boris's team never told him they were trying to get *Question Time* cancelled, and they kept him away from BBC London's

Tim Donovan, who had been covering City Hall long enough to know his stuff and pin Boris down. At Boris's campaign launch, where he accused me of increasing the council tax by £187, his team were furious when Donovan pointed out that 80 per cent of the increase had gone to pay for 7,000 extra police officers and 4,000 police community support officers. The truth was I increased the council tax by an average of 45p per week each year largely to pay for these police.

Each Sunday during the election Donovan interviewed the candidates in turn, with Boris scheduled for the final Sunday. Without warning Boris sent an assembly member in his place, claiming family commitments, even though at the very same time he was out campaigning in south-west London. That day in the *Sunday Times* AA Gill reported that I resembled the 'rheumy, blank confusion of the nursing home singalong' and my campaign team were like 'carers'. The day before polling Sarah Sands in the *Evening Standard* headlined 'Boris has a big heart … you don't have to be a Tory to vote for him'. Another story headlined 'Now 105 London business back Johnson' and had an interview with a Labour peer saying I was living in the past.

The weather on polling day was good, which was more than could be said for the final opinion polls. YouGov was closest with Boris 6 per cent ahead, others gave him a lead of up to 12 per cent. Because photographers always want pictures of the candidates voting, we trooped off to the polling station with Tom, Mia and Coco and three or four Labour Party activists, but some papers got confused and assumed they were all my children. As I worked my way across London in the 'Ken Fare Deal Express' bus with Eddie Izzard, Jo Brand and Roger Lloyd-Pack I couldn't believe the enthusiasm of the volunteers as they knocked on doors to get out the vote.

With so much at stake I had never felt such pressure in an election before. Most London families were thousands of pounds worse off since the banking crisis and all our policies were focused on helping out not just with fares but with energy bills and restoring the Education Maintenance Allowance for poorer students. It hit home when Ed Miliband came to the press screening of our party political broadcast. I had seen most of it but at the last minute the team had added a range of Londoners looking to camera and saying 'Come on Ken, London needs you'. The power of that desperate message moved me to tears and Ed gave me a reassuring pat on the back. I told the press it's 'because if I lose I lose the opportunity to help millions of ordinary Londoners for whom every day is now a terrible struggle … Boris has no understanding of what it is like to be an ordinary person struggling to put a hot meal on the table every night of the week. If I fail to do that, it's a guilt I carry to my grave. I want the chance to make life better for ordinary Londoners.' Ed chipped in, 'I think Ken has always been the underdog in this campaign. He has fought his way back into this race because of the power of his ideas. He is going to fight to the finish.'

Throughout the campaign I was haunted by the fact that if I didn't win millions of Londoners would be worse off, and I often had trouble sleeping. People still stop me on the street saying thanks for cutting fares when they were kids back in the '80s; pensioners wave their freedom pass and occasionally someone thanks me for rehousing them. I so wanted the chance to do all that again.

Because of the nastiness of the campaign turnout dropped from 45 per cent in 2008 to just 38 per cent, but it took all day to count the ballots. Simon phoned me early to say Labour members scrutinising the count could see Boris was narrowly ahead. I waited until the kids got back from school to tell them that Boris had won the election. Tom was quiet, but Mia, knowing I would now be at home, asked if we could get another puppy.

By the time I got to City Hall it was nearly 5 p.m. Simon said Boris had won by between 2 and 4 per cent. I told my team how sorry I was they wouldn't be part of a new administration. But as we waited for confirmation of the result there were rumours from the Tories of a growing panic that Boris might have lost. Crowley writes: 'the jollity didn't last long … it was beginning to look very close. The BBC then went from saying that Boris was sure to win, to describing the race as too close to call'. Crosby was particularly nervous. 'I don't think I've ever seen him so uncertain. He was tearing up the carpet as he paced up and down the room.'[13] Results from Bromley and Croydon showed Boris was down 17,000 and 7,000 votes respectively. Crosby told Crowley Boris might lose. Greenwich and Havering had him down by 7,000 and 13,000 votes and Crowley says the mood darkened further. Boris's head of media, Guto Harri, turned on Crosby saying if Boris lost it would be down to his negative campaign. Kate Bearman, former boss of Labour Friends of Israel, tweeted 'praying Ken's lost'.

The BBC now reported that it was possible I might win. Knowing this was rubbish I phoned Emma and my older children so they didn't get their hopes up. But panic worsened in the Tory team as we defeated two Tory assembly members and Boris's lead slipped to just 91,000 votes. Crowley continues: 'I was getting very negative messages from Crosby … Boris was fearing the worst and … some advisers had started packing up their belongings. It was entirely possible that Ken could … sneak in by the narrowest of margins. We braced ourselves for the worst. Boris's wife Marina … asked me what I thought. I gave her my honest assessment, no-one expected Ken to be so competitive at this stage.'[14]

As Boris's lead reached 107,000 Crosby cheered up and pizzas were brought in while Boris played whiff-whaff. Crosby told Crowley 'he thought we would just about make it'. But then the Enfield result had Boris's lead slip to just 90,000 and because the electricity had failed at the Brent and Harrow count three hours would pass before the final result was declared. Crowley continues: 'the wait was horrible. We ate, ordered wine and paced up and down. The empty punditry on TV grew tiresome … it was stomach churning.' As the Brent numbers came in Boris's lead dropped again. As they worked out how the second preferences would split, Crowley recalls, 'the raw numbers were heart stopping … we had a total lead of 324 votes. Everyone in the room gasped when we did the calculation.'[15]

Reading Crowley's book I wished I had been at the Tory camp. We had known for 12 hours that Boris had won, which said a lot for the organisation we built from the ground up. I still suffered the New Labour rule of no booze until after the result, but as the hours dragged on Jenny poked her head round the door and asked if I wanted a drink, so I rapidly decamped to the Greens.

Just before midnight we trooped on stage for the result to be announced. Boris had won by 1,054,811 to 992,273, a majority of 62,538 (3 per cent). My vote was 1 per cent less than the London-wide Labour Assembly vote, but Boris ran 11 per cent ahead of the Tories. Over half of his extra vote came from UKIP, BNP and other far-right parties and only a fifth were Labour defectors. Jenny, Brian and I groaned while Boris delivered an interminable repeat of his set campaign speech and didn't shake my hand. I followed on saying: '41 years ago almost to the day, I won my first election on a manifesto promising to build good council housing and introduce a free bus pass for pensioners. Now I've lived long enough to get one myself. Since then I have won 11 more elections and lost three but the one I most regret losing is this.'

I apologised to my supporters for failing to win and pointed out 'the incredible media battering' we had endured: 'These are the toughest times for 80 years. Londoners needed a mayor to help them get them through this very difficult period. They will continue to bear the pain of this recession without any help from City Hall.'

When I lost in 2008 it was straight back into campaigning and writing my autobiography, and my phone continued to ring all the time. This time was different, with nothing planned to keep me busy in the years ahead. On the Saturday I got up and replanted a tree that was falling over in the street and then started on my much neglected garden. As I pruned, weeded and dug I kept poring over the things I might have done to tip the balance, and was haunted by the fact that I wouldn't be able to help Londoners with their fares, rents and energy costs.

In a few constituencies New Labour MPs had sat on their hands and done nothing to get the vote out. For all my disagreements with Blair and Brown I always worked hard at their elections, as any Labour government is better than the Tories. I couldn't believe these Labour MPs were prepared to see Boris continue to pummel the poorest. Alan Sugar, who wasn't financially stretched, tweeted 'I seriously suggest NO ONE votes for Livingstone',[16] and Labour peers Winston and Desai both undermined the campaign with negative quotes in the *Evening Standard*.

In the run up to the election uber-Blairites had anonymously briefed the press that if we didn't win in London Ed would have to go, and so they did nothing to help. But although I lost Labour stormed to victory winning half the seats on the London Assembly, our second best local election result in London in 40 years. Labour's gains across Britain were a huge boost for Ed and the whingers went quiet.

Some Blairites were blaming me for losing even before the result, but Crowley says 'The truth is that Ken was popular enough to win, in that sense Labour had selected the right candidate … he would have beaten any other Conservative candidate easily.'[17] His view chimes with that of the *Guardian*'s Decca Aitkenhead, who after a long interview wrote: 'before we met, I had been all but convinced by Livingstone's critics that his time had passed – that he was too old, too tired, too dogmatic. And yet, spending time with him, he reminded me what a great mayor he was, and what a political phenomenon he still is, and I leave feeling unexpectedly inspired.'[18]

Some of my team fell out as recriminations bubbled over about what I had got wrong. Others felt that if the BBC hadn't cancelled the final debate and stopped *Today* interviewing the candidates that could have changed enough minds for us to win. Having worked for the BBC for seven years under a Tory government, Polly Toynbee wrote in the *Guardian* that the BBC 'operates not on bias but largely on fear. It tends to lean towards whoever frightens it most – and that's not Labour. When all the noise is from the Conservative dominated press and the Lynton Crosby war room, it loses its bearings without the balancing bullying that once came from Alistair Campbell and Peter Mandelson.'[19]

We didn't know who had taken the decisions but it had to be someone close to the top. Whether it was the Director General, Mark Thomson, or an underling, it certainly undermines Tory claims about the BBC's 'left-wing bias'. But as the Saville scandal erupted and Thomson said he knew nothing about his activities it is possible he also knew nothing about the cancellation of the debate. Either way it is an indictment of his competence as he allowed the BBC to betray its duty of impartiality. But the impact of the BBC was miniscule compared to the bias of newspaper owners who are the real villains.

Two thirds of papers people read are owned by a handful of billionaires: Murdoch, the Barclay Brothers, Lord Rothermere – all tax exiles. Amazingly an OFCOM report in 2013 found over 70 per cent of readers believe the *Telegraph* and the *Times* are trustworthy, with the *Daily Mail* on 43 per cent and the *Sun* on 30 per cent. Most of the press have always been partisan in elections, but it reached new lows in this campaign and was a warning of what was to come at the general election. When I came into politics the Tory press attacked Labour because of its policies, but since Murdoch dragged our standards down it has been all smears and personalities rather than issues and policy.

However much Blair, Boris and Cameron suck up to these billionaires their attitude to the politicians is typified by the *Evening Standard*'s owner Evgeny Lebedev naming his dog Boris. After the election the scale of their links became clear when it was revealed that Boris had spent two nights as a guest of Lebedev in Italy with his flights paid for. Two days later the editor of the *Standard*, Sarah Sands, paid for cars to take Boris from Farnborough airport to his home. Boris also failed to declare that he had a secret dinner with Rupert Murdoch after the police started investigating phone hacking.

When I was leader of the GLC there were some smears – Tory Central Office circulated the rumour that I had been sodomised by six men in an East End pub one Friday night, and *Private Eye* was told Gaddafi had put £200,000 in my 'secret Swiss bank account' – but mainly I was attacked because of my support for public services, negotiating with the IRA, and fighting racism, sexism and homophobia. After six months my poll rating sank to 18 per cent and I was assaulted three times on the streets but I didn't give in. With the passage of time we won the political debate, and when the GLC was abolished in 1986 the majority of Londoners supported all our policies except gay and lesbian rights, and even the support for that was over 40 per cent.

During the 2008 mayoral election campaign Andrew Gilligan, then working at the *Evening Standard*, wrote endless headline stories alleging corruption and fraud in my administration. When Boris won he appointed the Tory Patience Wheatcroft to chair a committee of enquiry comprised of Tory council leaders and accountants. They took three months to report that they could find no evidence of cronyism or corruption. I had referred the allegations to the police, but after an investigation lasting two and a half years the fraud squad found no evidence to bring a single charge against any of the people who had been smeared by Gilligan and the *Evening Standard*.

Given his record I was amazed that other papers took up Gilligan's tax smear without checking. The enquiry into the death of Dr David Kelly revealed Gilligan had over-egged his claims that Alistair Campbell 'sexed up' the WMD dossier. Disgracefully Gilligan revealed Kelly's identity to Lib Dem MP David Chidgey, starting a witch-hunt that led to Kelly's suicide. His then colleague at the *Telegraph*, Elizabeth Day, described Gilligan as 'a man of contradictions … insecure yet arrogant … over-indulgent, gentle yet controlling … who sets his own rules and lives by them with a desperate eccentricity'. He usually turned up late, working alone through the night 'filing late copy … incredibly arrogant and [with] an unshakeable belief in his own ability'.[20] Boris had given Gilligan a job after the Hutton enquiry and then the Barclay Brothers employed him as the *Telegraph*'s London editor, so he could spend the years up to 2012 attacking me and his other obsession, Islam.

Initially under the editorship of Geordie Greig the *Evening Standard* became more upbeat, but he quit before the election and Sarah Sands, a family friend of the Johnsons, took over. A sign of what was to come was the *Evening Standard* of 26th January reporting 'there are rumours Ken is tired and drinks too heavily'.

Occasionally a council candidate registers fraudulent postal votes. The corruption is well reported and they go to prison. But how can we have free and fair elections when a few media barons can fix the outcome of an election by lying with impunity about the parties and candidates they oppose while boosting those who protect their tax dodging? Commercial radio and television have a reasonable record of impartiality and there is no reason why the regulator OFCOM, who monitors them, should not also do the same for the BBC and our national newspapers.

Murdoch has always had access to prime ministers. He got Thatcher to drop the rules that prevented him acquiring the *Times* as well as the *Sun*, and as a reward for Murdoch's support in the 2010 election Cameron promised to change the rule preventing him from gaining full control of Sky television. While the police were investigating the phone hacking scandal Boris's deputy mayor lobbied the police three times to ease off on the enquiry.

Given the unremitting media attention I had as GLC leader and mayor it was appalling to watch the papers ignore Boris's record as mayor. With a few exceptions, like the *Guardian*, the papers covered Boris's photo ops but didn't report the TfL surplus or his failure to build housing, whilst he raised fares to the highest in the world. In our debates Boris promised to tackle air pollution but with the election over he worked with the far-right Italian Northern League to lobby the EU against its air quality standards. He could have had measures to reduce pollution in place by 2012 but has put it off until 2020. This means 35,000 people may die prematurely because of his failure to act. In 2015 a report by King's College London estimated the figure to be 9,500 premature deaths per year, which means Boris's inaction could contribute to 75,000 deaths.

When he announced that he was returning to Parliament at the 2015 election Boris claimed he had taken 'the job of mayor to gain administrative experience'. Yet the truth is Boris dumps the work on his deputy mayors, and when a photo appeared of him standing before his desk after five years as mayor I noticed everything was exactly as I had left it. He hadn't even moved the pot containing pens and pencils. The LSE's Tony Travers said 'in some ways Boris's policies are Ken-lite. Boris, luckily for him, has ended up cutting the ribbons.' Travers continued: 'he won't be seen as someone who profoundly changed the city. You can well imagine in 100 years time people will be talking about Boris bikes ... but no one will remember who Boris was.'[21] The next mayor elected in 2016 will have to move quickly to tackle the problems of transport overcrowding and the housing crisis.

But none of this has dented Boris's rising popularity. By May 2013 polls showed 65 per cent of Londoners thought he was doing well or fairly well – including 55 per cent of Labour voters! Those who knew Boris best take a different view. Max Hastings, who as editor of the *Telegraph* recruited him, said in the *Daily Mail*:

Most politicians are ambitious and ruthless, but Boris is a gold-medal egomaniac. I would not trust him with my wife nor – from painful experience – my wallet ... He is not a man to believe in, to trust or respect, save as a superlative exhibitionist. He is bereft of judgement, loyalty and discretion. Only in the star-crazed frivolous Britain of the 21st century could such a man have risen so high, and he is utterly unfit to go higher still.[22]

Similarly, Sonia Purnell, who was his deputy during his years reporting from Brussels, wrote in the *Sunday Times*:

No one else had worked at such close quarters with him ... I had observed that under a well cultivated veneer of disorganisation lay not so much a streak of aspiration as a torrent of almost frightening focus and drive. He pumped others for information, guidance and contacts but did not reciprocate and was obsessively secretive. Sometimes he could even be downright obstructive ... The wife of one of his Bullingdon Club cohorts said that her husband would 'not speak about Boris, even off the record, as he is frightened of what he might do back'. A lot of people are.[23]

In the *Guardian* Purnell wrote:

Johnson is rarely a friend. In fact, although many might describe themselves as a pal, they are usually mistaken. Johnson does not have friends merely interests. Most admit they have rarely if ever conducted a lengthy conversation with Johnson; he is not one to share a pint at the pub with a mate ... It is as if he erects the highest walls around himself to avoid any of us really getting to know him. What does he fear we would find out if we did? Nor does he show loyalty to those who have helped him most but are no longer in a position to do more ... To those who have worked closely with Johnson, his outbursts of temper are notorious; even his sister, Rachel, describes his approach to those who dare to criticise him as Sicilian ... Boris Johnson is unparalleled in politics in terms of self-promotion and even occasionally cheering us up. He is hugely clever and politically astute but after more than four years as mayor he has yet to prove himself in action, let alone as a contender to be prime minister.[24]

Boris benefited from opening projects I started but excluded me from any visit to the Olympic site until after the election. Fortunately Danny Boyle had been kind enough to take me through the opening ceremony in case I won. The big increase in public investment I secured from Blair and Brown helped London's economy recover from the recession. But Boris has not started projects which the next mayor will open and which are vital if London is to succeed. Boris has only two projects as his legacy: the cable car to nowhere and the Orbit restaurant in the Olympic Park.

CHAPTER FOUR

Rebuilding the Party, Rebuilding Britain

by Ken Livingstone

My whole life changed following my defeat in the 2012 mayoral election. After a lifetime rushing from meeting to meeting I had time to be a house husband and look after the gardens of two of my neighbours who were disabled. While I was mayor, my partner Emma put her own ambitions on hold to focus on Tom and Mia. Like me Emma hadn't gone to university but now she could. By 2015 she had a first-class honours degree, a postgraduate teaching qualification, and had embarked on a new career as a teacher in Hackney.

While working on my neighbour's gardens I kept going over in my head what Blair had got wrong and what we needed to learn if we were to go into the next election with a credible economic strategy. In my lifetime only two elections have changed Britain: Labour under Attlee in 1945 and the Tories under Thatcher in 1979. In both the winning party won the economic debate, so even when they lost office their opponents continued their policies. Attlee inherited the largest debt in British history, two and a half times the size of today's. Instead of tipping Britain into austerity to pay off the debt, Labour built a full-employment economy to generate the growth, wealth and taxes that could pay off the debt and give my generation the best quality of life in human history. Over the next six years Labour switched the economy from wartime production back to manufacturing, recaptured many of our lost export markets and created the welfare state of which the jewel is the NHS. When the Tories returned to power they continued Labour's strategy.

Harold Macmillan's diaries – which are very honest as he never intended they should be published – give us a remarkable insight into the 13 years of Tory rule. Macmillan was genuinely worried as unemployment rose over 2.5 per cent, and thought it was a crisis when it reached 4 per cent in the early 1960s. He tried strategies to protect our industrial base and involve the trade unions. His generation of Tory leaders had fought alongside the working class in both World Wars and respected their courage and patriotism, unlike today's Eton and Bullingdon Club clique that views working-class culture as just *Benefit Street* or *Shameless*.

Thatcher won in 1979 with a strategy to break the trade unions, deregulate the financial sector, cut taxes and roll back the state. As with Labour in 1945 she won the economic argument, so when Tony Blair came to power 18 years later he believed it was his 'job to build on what she achieved, not roll it back'. Had he told us this when he was running for Labour leader the outcome would have been very different.

Thatcher won the debate with the support from Murdoch's empire, the *Telegraph* and the *Mail*, who rewrote history by demonising the post-war period of Attlee and Macmillan and depicting the 1970s as the decade 'when the lights went out' with Britain on the verge of collapse. When Thatcher died, Cameron said 'she did not just lead Britain, she saved it'. However, the *Economist*, a key promoter of neoliberalism, in six pages analysing Thatcher's legacy, did not mention the rate of economic growth or levels of investment. Had they done so it would have been clear that in the years since Thatcher we have not achieved the levels of growth and investment that we did in the years before. In the 30 years before Thatcher the

UK economy grew by nearly 150 per cent; in the following 30 years it was barely 100 per cent.

When I told this to David Mellor (my co-host on our weekly LBC radio programme) he was shocked. Like most people he believed that neoliberalism had worked. Labour and the Tories blaming each other for the mess we are in is inane. The truth is we are in this mess because Thatcher, Blair and Osborne followed the same economic policy. The same is true of the American economy under Reagan, Clinton, Bush senior and junior, and Obama.

In December 2014 the OECD published evidence that Britain's economy would have been over 20 per cent larger if the gap between the richest and the poorest had not widened so dramatically in the years since Thatcher was elected.

The problems of the 1970s weren't caused by public spending or the trade unions but by the Saudis, who used their dominance in OPEC to force through a fourfold increase in the price of oil in 1973. The year before, Germany had achieved its highest ever level of investment (25 per cent of GDP) and Britain had peaked at 20 per cent. In the 1980s, the decade of the so-called Reagan boom, America's economy grew by no more than it had in the '70s, with its oil crisis and hyper-inflation. Britain was the same, but when in 1992 the BBC's *Panorama* produced a programme demonstrating this, BBC bosses banned it from being shown.

Another reason Britain did not do better economically is because we increased military spending as the Cold War took hold, spending vast sums on military adventures which caused a recurring balance of payments crisis. Initially France made the same error, but in 1962 De Gaulle cut military spending by 2 per cent of GDP and by the end of that decade France had overtaken Britain economically. Germany, the most successful economy in Europe, spends half as much as we do on its military, allowing more to be invested in research and infrastructure, even though it is closer to Russia than we are.

Over the last 100 years the only periods in which Britain's manufacturing sector grew as a share of the economy was in the 1930s, when government froze interest rates at 2 per cent which led to a manufacturing boom, and when Attlee's post-war government kept interest rates at 2 per cent as it rebuilt our manufacturing base. Financial institutions lobbied the 1951 Tory government to increase interest rates, boosting the profitability of the financial sector which was then just 2 per cent of the British economy. In the 1950s Britain's share of manufacturing exports started falling as we fell behind German, Dutch and Japanese levels of investment.

Following Thatcher's deregulation of the financial industry in 1986, banks and hedge funds flocked to London where they could gamble and take risks in ways that were illegal in their home countries. By 2007 the UK financial sector had grown to 8 per cent of the economy.

But the increase in jobs in the financial sector took its toll on manufacturing. Under Chancellors Ken Clarke and Gordon Brown interest rates were usually 2 per cent higher than in Germany. Why would a manufacturing firm build a plant in Britain if it had to pay substantially more in interest on the money it borrowed? Those firms that did come to Britain did so because lower wage levels outweighed the cost of high interest rates.

In 1979, 30 per cent of our economy was in manufacturing, which employed 6.8 million people. By the time Thatcher left office it was 11 per cent, employing 2.5 million people – 4.3 million jobs wiped out. Since the 2007–8 crisis the banks have cut lending to manufacturing firms from 3.3 per cent of their total lending to just 1.3 per cent.

Britain's economy was built by Victorian entrepreneurs who invested, but today entrepreneurs prefer a quick return.

They make money persuading the government to privatise utilities or allow them to rip off our pensions. Short-termism will not rebalance the economy and give all people a chance to achieve their potential. Germany didn't allow banks to become masters of its economy, instead they serve its overall needs. Germany has a manufacturing sector twice the size of ours, and by providing skilled jobs for the working class has a youth unemployment rate just one third of ours.

In 1997 government debt was 42 per cent of GDP. It was 43 per cent in 2007 but the bail-out of the banks had pushed it up to 53 per cent by the 2010 election. Osborne's austerity cuts pushed us back into recession and now government debt is over 80 per cent of GDP. The solution is not to fiddle with cautious incremental measures until we are overwhelmed by another economic crisis. Like Attlee in 1945 we need a game-changing economic strategy that sets a path of sustainable growth as Jeremy Corbyn is proposing.

Investment is the most important factor in growth, outweighing all other factors combined. Britain became an economic superpower in the nineteenth century because we were the first country in history to invest 7 per cent of our GDP a year. America's dominance of the twentieth century came as they raised investment to 19 per cent, and West Germany led the post-war reconstruction of Europe achieving 25 per cent in 1973. Japan became the second largest economy in the world after investing 38 per cent of its GDP and China will overtake the USA because it is investing 46 per cent.

By April 2014 I was ready to write to Ed Miliband with a set of economic proposals which I believed would give him a chance of winning the economic debate at the 2015 general election. Given that the Tories, with the support of the press barons, had tarred Labour with spending and borrowing too much, I asked Ed 'how can we increase investment today without taking on more debt?' In my letter I said the answer lay in the success of the Bank of England's Quantitative Easing programme, which had rescued the financial sector without fuelling inflation (contrary to the predictions of neoliberal economists). The Bank created £375 billion of new money, equivalent to 25 per cent of GDP, without borrowing a penny. The Bank could do the same to fund infrastructure, which would improve our competitiveness, attract private investment and create millions of new jobs. The proposals I put to Ed included the following:

We could build 150,000 homes a year for rent. These homes would remain the property of the Bank while being managed by councils and housing associations. We should ensure a good social mix with some tenants eventually buying their homes. But if or when they move they should be sold back to the council or housing associations to help others off the waiting list.

We should commit to HS2, Crossrail 2, a Liverpool to Leeds high-speed rail link to revive the Northern economies, and extensive tram and light rail schemes, which would also remain the property of the Bank while being managed by Network Rail, TfL and new regional authorities.

Laying down a fibre optic cable system linking every home, school, college and business would enable us to match the speed of broadband access in much of East Asia and lead to the creation of hundreds of thousands of new jobs in addition to those created by installing the system. This would be owned by the Bank with firms paying for use of the network.

We should address climate change by insulating all buildings. The insulation could not be owned by the Bank but it would be paid back by savings in energy bills until the cost was recovered, after which customers would benefit. The Bank should also fund climate change research and the start-up costs of firms dealing with solutions to climate change.

Just as the Bank will eventually sell the £375 billion of bonds it has bought as the economy improves, so it could sell its housing, transport and fibre optic investments, but I would prefer them to be sold to British pension funds rather than repeat the mistakes of privatisation.

This would be our biggest ever programme of public investment, creating full employment within five years. It would involve not a penny of borrowing and no increase in national debt. It might not be possible to repeat QE in a second term as in a full-employment economy it could lead to inflation. In a growing, full-employment economy deficits are manageable, but the Tories have won the deficit debate so Labour has to show it won't increase borrowing.

We can also freeze energy prices, fares and rents (and extend leases to protect tenants from unsavoury landlords). This would put money into the pockets of those most in need without increasing the deficit, which would fuel growth in demand and encourage private sector investment.

We should reduce the benefits bill by moving from the minimum wage to the living wage over two years. We could cover the cost to employers via a tax rebate funded by a crackdown on tax avoidance and evasion which some estimates put as high as £150 billion, equivalent to 10 per cent of GDP (a quarter of the government's budget!).

We should abolish the business rate and replace it with a tax on turnover, which would be as impossible for Google, Starbucks and the others to avoid paying as it is easy for them to avoid the business rate. The tax could be set at a level that excludes small and medium sized enterprises. This would focus the minds of corporate tax avoiders on the threat that a turnover tax could also replace corporation tax unless they end the culture of avoidance.

These policies would allow us to rid Britain of debt within 20 years.

Some corporations might complain, but dividend payments are currently at their highest levels in history, investment at a post-war low, and wages have been cut from two thirds of GDP to just over half. These policies would benefit corporations as the economy grows.

The faint-hearted will consider all this too radical, but it is a fair balance of Keynesian and monetarist thinking that would allow Labour to go into the next election promising no increase in borrowing and a big cut in Britain's debt burden. We could achieve full employment and the highest ever levels of investment. After the failure of the Thatcher-Reagan experiment Britain has the chance to set a new economic agenda which would be copied by other nations as they saw its benefits.

Weeks turned into months without any response to my letter from Ed's office. His staff said they were considering it and that it had been passed to Ed Balls. No one was specific but there were hints of tensions between the two Eds on economic strategy. It was only when Labour's NEC and the shadow cabinet met to agree our election manifesto that Balls revealed his opposition to my proposals, dismissing the use of quantitative easing to fund investment in infrastructure as 'just another form of borrowing'.

Just as disappointing was the meeting's line on Trident. I pointed out that the manifesto's reference to our 'independent' nuclear weapons system was based on a fallacy. I was doing a paper-round in 1962 when Macmillan and Kennedy met to agree that, since Britain could no longer afford to develop its own nuclear weapons we would, in the future, buy them from the USA. The following morning all the papers I pushed through letter boxes had headlines denouncing Macmillan for giving up our genuinely independent nuclear weapons, yet all parties parrot the line that we still have an independent system. Almost everyone present at the NEC meeting had a brief laugh and then nodded the lie through. I didn't laugh as I'd been there before, back in the run up to the 1992 election when Kinnock got the party to drop its opposition to getting rid of our nukes 'because we can't win the election otherwise'. It made no difference as we still lost the election. We need to tell the voters the truth. Not only is it not independent, it is very expensive at £20 billion to build the delivery system and then £80 billion to run it for the next 30 years. That works out at about £5,000 for every family in Britain – enough to build half a million new homes and create nearly a million new jobs.

One of Jeremy Corbyn's recent decisions has been to make me joint chair of the review commission looking at our defence policy. No sooner had he done this than the Tories confessed that the cost of building four new nuclear submarines had risen to £31 billion and they had set aside another £10 billion as the cost could rise. It was also revealed in the *Guardian* that a report to the Pentagon in 2013, following research by scientists in the US military, warned that Russia and China had developed the ability to incapacitate our defences by a cyber-attack hacking into the control system.[1] They estimated it would cost tens of billions to develop a system to prevent such a cyber-attack. While many people will say yes if asked whether we should have nuclear weapons, they might change their minds when told what is going to cost them in income tax.

No sooner was that NEC meeting over than a new introduction was added to the manifesto, which caused despair and anger amongst many of Ed Miliband's closest advisers who had been kept in the dark. The new introduction was soon being dismissed as 'austerity-lite', or even worse, as 'Tory-lite'. We did not lose the election because we were too left-wing but because we did not present a credible alternative to the Tories.

With the election underway I wasn't going to criticise Labour's timid austerity-lite strategy but I was appalled by the lack of imagination or confidence in challenging the Tories' economic failure. Whenever I raised the use of quantitative easing for investment with business groups they all thought it was a good idea. When talking to financial journalists they could see no problem with such a strategy.

I only campaigned in key Tory and Liberal marginal seats. Although the mood of activists was upbeat, all over the country I found angry working-class people who would once have been traditional Labour supporters asking what the last Labour government did for them as good working-class jobs continued to disappear and Blair continued Thatcher's ban on building council homes for their children. They weren't saying we were too left-wing but they were voting for UKIP or the SNP because of the last Labour government's failure to provide them with real opportunities.

Still, I was impressed by Ed Miliband's confident performance and buoyed by the polls. The only bad moment came when Ed fluffed his response to a question in a TV debate about whether or not Labour had spent and borrowed too much. The day before the election all NEC members got an invite to come to Labour HQ for the expected victory party after the polls closed. As I was due to do interviews in the Westminster media compound at 7 a.m. the following morning, I skipped the party and settled down in front of the TV waiting for the exit poll.

Like almost everybody else in Labour's team I was devastated as the poll showed comfortable Tory gains. Opinion polls had never been so wildly wrong in any previous election. The result was so unexpected and depressing that when I arrived at the media compound every other Labour representative had failed to turn up and I spent two hours filling in for all the no-shows. The mood was even worse than after Labour's unexpected defeat at the 1992 election, but I kept reminding my interviewers that five years later Labour was elected in a landslide and held power for 13 years. I also pointed out we had not lost because we were too left-wing but because we did not have a coherent alternative economic strategy. In fact the only region in Britain where the swing to Labour was big enough to put Ed in Number 10 was London, where the reputation of the Labour Party has been strong for nearly 34 years, since the 1981 GLC election.

I hoped Ed would stay on and fight back because the Tories would soon be deeply unpopular as Osborne pushed the economy back into recession and started cutting public services back to the level of the 1930s. Sadly, Ed resigned and immediately the old Blairites seized on our defeat to try and push Labour to the right. Their claim was that only Blair could have won the 1997 election and that was because he moved the party to the right. But as Bob Worcester, Britain's leading pollster for over 40 years, showed in his analysis of the 1997 election result, John Smith and Neil Kinnock would both have won easily. Labour's two subsequent victories in 2001 and 2005 were more to do with the Tories' civil war over Europe than any great support for Blairism. In fact, Labour's vote plummeted in 2001 as turnout at the election slumped to the lowest ever in our history and over 60 per cent of Labour Party members resigned or allowed their membership to lapse.

When I joined the Labour Party in 1969 it had half a million members and up to 20 people would gather each month at their local branch, planning campaigns and discussing what Labour's policies should be. Each of those wards could send policy motions, via their local constituency management committee, which would be debated at the Labour Party conference. These policies formed the basis of Labour's election manifesto and I found these meetings exhilarating. It was a chance for ordinary people to have a say in British politics, but from the moment Tony Blair became Labour leader he started to remove the democratic structures and instead devise policy with a small group appointed by himself. Conference was denied the right to vote on motions and turned into a series of photo opportunities and PR events.

The right of local Labour parties to select whoever they wanted as their candidate for Parliament was also withdrawn. Parties could now only choose from a list of approved candidates who had spent a weekend locked away in a hotel where Blairite officials weeded out anyone who was genuinely Labour. The composition of the Parliamentary Labour Party changed rapidly. As already discussed in Chapter 2, the most extreme example came when Blair created the London mayoralty. Two hundred and thirty Labour Party members applied to stand for the 25 seats on the London Assembly but 136 were barred from standing by a small committee of party officials on the grounds that they 'lacked life experience'.

The transformation of the party was funded by big business. Lord David Sainsbury gave a quarter of a million pounds a year to Progress, an organisation run by uber-Blairites. Sainsbury had been director of finance at the family firm when on 23 October 1981, along with representatives of GEC, Tate & Lyle, Beechams, Ladbrokes and Cadbury Schweppes, they agreed to fund the Aims of Industry campaign for the abolition of the GLC. Now he and the British Venture Capital Association poured money into the Progress organisation to change the Labour Party and make it subservient to corporate interests.[2]

When I became the leader of the GLC, the London Labour Party was a vibrant organisation which had complete freedom to draw up Labour's manifesto for the GLC elections at an annual meeting with over 600 delegates present. In the run up to the 2000 mayoral election the London Labour Party conference had been reduced to just a few dozen members and the drafting of the manifesto had been completely removed from their hands.

It wasn't only in London that party democracy was wiped out, it happened everywhere. Having created a Welsh Assembly, Blair blocked the Welsh Labour Party from selecting Rhodri Morgan, who was the overwhelming choice of party members, to be their leader and imposed Alun Michael, who was rejected by every single Welsh constituency as their local candidate and had to be imposed by HQ via the top-up list.

To prevent local parties electing independent-minded members to Labour's NEC, Blair changed the rules so that MPs could only be elected by the now Blairite-dominated Parliamentary Labour Party. I was elected in the last NEC elections before this rule change and couldn't believe how much the NEC had already been turned into a mere rubber stamp. When I challenged the chair's ruling I was told the rules had been changed and this was no longer allowed.

What Blair did in gutting the Labour Party was a disgrace to democracy. But at least as damaging was his approach to economic policy. Like most MPs economic policy was not his main interest. When I was elected to Parliament I decided to concentrate on the economy, and for two years John Ross, a socialist economist, came into the House of Commons two or three times a week to explain to me what was happening in the British and world economies. Over those two years I gained the confidence to speak on economic issues, and John and I began to produce the *Socialist Economic Bulletin*. Most Labour MPs focus on housing, the NHS, human rights, or challenging racism, sexism and homophobia. They hope someone else will deal with the economy.

Lacking any real understanding of economics, Blair was overawed by bankers and hedge fund managers while denying the trade unions a say in drawing up our economic policy. He believed the neoliberal lie that Thatcher and Reagan had saved Britain and America by breaking the power of trade unions, cutting taxes on corporations and deregulating the financial sector.

In my letter to Ed Miliband I had pointed out that neoliberal policies had not equalled the levels of growth and investment achieved in the post-war Keynesian era, and far from Keynesian strategy being anti-business it had provided an environment in which businesses flourished. Even with my left-wing beliefs, as mayor I was able to assemble a coalition of big businesses, trade unions and community groups to agree a 20-year economic strategy for London based on investment in our transport system, providing the spur to attract private sector investment. Over the next 15 years London overtook New York, Hong Kong and Singapore and became the only region in Europe to match US productivity levels. Why do so many politicians continue to subscribe to the failed Thatcherite strategy when it takes just a few minutes of accessing data on the Treasury's own website to show how it failed?.

Then there is the role of American foreign policy and how that intersects with corporate power. As Oliver Stone's *Untold History of the United States* makes graphically clear, it was America that organised the overthrow of democratically elected governments in Brazil, Chile, Argentina and other countries around the world. The greatest tragedy was the war in Vietnam. When Ho Chi Min announced the independence of Vietnam as Japan surrendered in 1945, he asked for US support and his statement of independence strongly echoed the American Declaration of Independence. If the US State Department had had a better understanding of the history of the endless conflicts between Vietnam and China over the centuries, they could have avoided the subsequent 30 years of warfare that led to millions of Vietnamese casualties.

The reality is that two years before the end of the Second World War corporate leaders in America were already planning for a Cold War. These people included Charles

Wilson, president of General Motors, Edward Stettinius, the chairman of US Steel, Wall Street's James Forrestal, and Averell Harriman, the son of a railroad baron who was ambassador to the USSR. Several big US businesses feared the popularity of Stalin and wanted a Cold War in order to continue massive spending on arms. In August 1943, the OSS (forerunner of the CIA) warned that 'peace will not be long enduring, until either our way of thought and life, or somebody else's, becomes general and controlling in the world ... we are a nation of nations peculiarly well equipped for the undertaking.'[3]

President Roosevelt was looking for a post-war consensus with Stalin based on providing massive financial aid, totalling $10 billion, and giving Stalin an assurance that the European countries bordering the USSR would not have hostile governments. Tragically with Roosevelt's death the corporations got their way, and 40 years of a ruinously expensive Cold War followed.

The same deception and dishonesty in much of the media is now applied to the so-called threat from Islam. Nowhere in the *Telegraph*, *Mail* or Murdoch's press are we ever told that the origin of Islamic terrorism lies in decades of funding by the West and its ally Saudi Arabia. In 1955 Harold Macmillan wrote in his diary of his concern that the oil money flowing into Saudi Arabia was being used to fund the spread of the extremist Wahhabi strand of Islam. He wrote: 'The Saudis ... are bribing everyone, right and left, and are turning the whole Arab world upside down. If something could be done to stop this it would be the biggest possible contribution to peace.'[4] A CIA report in 2003 revealed that the Saudis had spent at least $2 billion a year for over 30 years spreading their pernicious fundamentalism.

The USA and Britain also funded and armed Muslim terror groups in the border areas of the USSR during the Cold War. The most shocking example came in July 1979 when

President Carter agreed to supply arms to the Mujahideen in Afghanistan as they launched attacks against the pro-Soviet government in Kabul. Carter was told by the CIA that this would provoke a Russian military intervention which would become 'their Vietnam'. It never occurred to anyone in the US government that once these fanatics had driven the Russians out of Afghanistan they might then turn on us. In agreeing to supply arms to the Mujahideen, Carter lit the fuse that led to 9/11. Similarly, Tony Blair was warned by our security services that intervening in Afghanistan would make us a target for terrorist attacks, as eventually happened on 7/7.

Still today our governments lie about the causes of terrorism. Endless Western interventions in the Middle East have never produced a good outcome, from the overthrowing of the democratically elected government of Iran in 1953, because they had nationalised the foreign-owned oil wells, all the way through to Cameron telling the House of Commons that deposing Gaddafi would create a better situation for the Libyan people. Full details of the UK's direct involvement in the spread of Islamic terrorism can be found in Mark Curtis's book *Dirty Wars*.

We can't have a real democracy unless people are able to read the truth in our newspapers. Very little is revealed to readers about the growing influence of corporate power in undermining democracy. One shocking example was the revelation of an internal memo from Chase Manhattan written in January 1995 about the politics of Mexico, which they feared threatened corporate interests. The bank warned that 'we will need to consider carefully whether or not to allow opposition victories if fairly won at the ballot box … the government will have to eliminate the Zapatistas to demonstrate their effective control of the national territory and security policy'.[5]

The secretive negotiations between the EU and the USA on the Transatlantic Trade and Investment Partnership (TTIP) represent the latest drive to extend corporate power. This treaty plans to remove many of Europe's regulations which protect workers' rights and the environment and will allow a secret panel of corporate lawyers to overrule parliamentary laws by fining governments for lost profits because of the restrictions applied by the EU. An indication of what is to come was revealed when EU plans to ban chemicals linked to autism, cancer and male infertility from being added to pesticides were dropped. Warnings from the USA that these regulations could derail the TTIP treaty caused the EU to drop the proposals even though there is clear evidence that these chemicals lead to obesity, IQ loss and damage to the genitals of baby boys.

Although I had real respect for Ed Miliband for his decision to admit the war in Iraq was wrong and for his stand against getting involved in Syria, he also needed to admit that Labour had not been radical enough in tackling our economic problems. But he was surrounded by so many Blairite MPs who refused to acknowledge that the Labour government had been too cautious. One of the reasons Labour didn't go into the last election with a commitment to use quantitative easing to fund the modernisation of Britain's infrastructure was the Blairites refusal to accept that giving independence to the Bank of England was a mistake. No one in their right mind would design a motor car in which one person operated the steering wheel while someone else managed the brake and accelerator. A system in which planning the direction of the economy is split between a government that controls the budget and an independent bank that controls interest rates and the money supply is a similar recipe for disaster.

Devolving control over interest rates and the money supply to a body dominated by individuals from the financial sector guarantees a continuing neglect of the need to build a better balanced economy. During Labour's leadership election

Jeremy Corbyn's support for using QE for investment was denounced by his rivals as a threat to the independence of the Bank of England. But the Bank had done fine in the preceding 250 years in which it was always subordinate to the economic strategy of the government of the day.

For its first 90 years the Labour Party's rules were open and always allowed a left-wing candidate to contest leadership elections. All that was required was that the candidate be nominated by two MPs. But after Tony Benn's leadership challenge in 1988 against Neil Kinnock the NEC rule was changed. In future, a leadership contender would have to be nominated by 20 per cent of Labour MPs. At that NEC meeting I reminded Kinnock that when Wilson retired in 1976 six MPs contested the election and that would have been impossible under this rule, but the trade union members lined up behind Kinnock and pushed it through, while only Tony Benn, Dennis Skinner and myself opposed it. That autumn the trade union block vote pushed the change through conference.

Inevitably, when Kinnock resigned after our defeat at the 1992 general election, Bernie Grant and I got barely a quarter of the MPs we needed to nominate us for the posts of leader and deputy. Two years later, after John Smith died, the Socialist Campaign Group kicked around the idea of my running with Jeremy Corbyn as deputy, but again we had no chance of getting enough nominations. For two decades, leadership elections became little more than a rubber stamp for the establishment candidate until the defeat of David Miliband in 2010. Because Ed Miliband's victory was based on his big lead in the trade union voting block, Blairites immediately started pressing to reduce trade union influence in future leadership elections.

The Blairites claimed victory when the party changed the rules and removed the trade union block vote. In future, trade union members could only vote as individuals. The Blairites also persuaded the party to allow members of the public to take part in leadership elections after paying just £3. In effect, future leadership elections would be more like the open primary system by which American parties select their presidential candidate. Following Ed Miliband's resignation, Cooper, Kendall and Burnham were off and running, but the first two weeks of the leadership election were breathtakingly dull. People were stopping me on the street to complain about how the candidates were so 'boring' and 'all the same'. This may be why several Labour MPs agreed to nominate Jeremy Corbyn, in order to generate a more engaging debate around the issues.

At first no one, including Jeremy, believed he could win, but everything changed when deputy leader Harriet Harman ruled that Labour MPs would not vote against the Tories' benefits cuts. Jeremy refused to go along with this disgraceful decision and led dozens of Labour MPs into the 'No' lobby while his three opponents abstained.

That moment changed everything. People rushed to join up in order to vote for Jeremy, and not just because of that one vote, but because he was the only candidate with a coherent alternative to George Osborne's austerity strategy. Jeremy was advocating that 'people's quantitative easing' could be used to invest in modernising our economy without increasing borrowing, and services like health and education could be improved not by increasing taxes on working and middle-class voters, but by cracking down on the tax dodging of the likes of Google, Starbucks and Amazon.

Jeremy's bold and coherent economic strategy electrified the leadership election. A surge of new members took Labour's membership back to the level before Blair with a high proportion of under 30s joining. At Jeremy's rallies the turn-outs dwarfed those of his rivals as for the first time in many years Labour seemed to be promising a better future for all. As the polls showed Jeremy's lead increasing, 'New'

Labour MPs were bewildered. After 21 years parroting the line that 'only Blair could have won' they were being swept aside by a tide of hope and optimism from the general public, many of who had voted UKIP, Green or SNP, or had not even bothered to vote because of Labour's 'austerity-lite' policy in the general election.

Blair's intervention only increased Jeremy's support as hundreds of thousands voted to object to years of New Labour caution. The Tory press and some Labour MPs started predicting a civil war in the party, a return to the 1980s and even another SDP type split with dozens of MPs defecting. As Labour's conference following Jeremy's election as leader got under way, the doom-mongers could not have been proved more wrong. Jeremy had been able to create a broad-based shadow cabinet with only a few embittered Blairites refusing to take part.

After years of listening to most Labour MPs toeing the New Labour line the media couldn't get its head around the fact that Jeremy had restored the democratic principle that MPs should be free to say what they believe without the threat of discipline or expulsion. After years of dull, boring PR conferences, Labour had come alive again.

There was a return to the 1980s, but it was made by the Tories and their press allies, not the Labour Party. As the *Mail*, *Sun* and *Telegraph* ran screaming 'Red Jeremy' headlines, alongside Cameron's smears that he was a threat to our economy and our national security, it was like re-living the attacks on the Labour GLC and myself in 1981 all over again. Back then it took just three months of lies and smears to push my poll ratings down to 18 per cent. But like then, Jeremy has not given in to the onslaught and turned tail, but pressed ahead with his changes.

Four billionaires – Rupert Murdoch, Lord Rothermere, and Sirs David and Frederick Barclay – own the newspapers that the majority of us read. As all are tax dodgers they will do anything to prevent the election of a government that would make them pay their fair share of tax, so the lies and smears will continue. But Jeremy has shown his ability to overcome the Tory press by engaging directly with voters over the internet.

In the months and years to come Jeremy's Labour Party will become an open and campaigning movement that engages with the people, which is our only way to win. The Momentum movement created by the newly inspired members has launched its first campaign to defeat Cameron's new laws designed to make it more difficult for poorer people to get onto the electoral register. These laws have been rushed through so that millions of non-Tory voters can be thrown off the registers before the boundary review begins. If Cameron succeeds then dozens of Labour seats will be abolished, potentially ensuring a permanent Tory majority in the House of Commons. Jeremy's win gives us a chance to defeat this outrageous rigging of elections, as well as giving people the chance to elect a government that will govern in the interests of all Britons, not just the richest 1 per cent.

Mine is the luckiest generation in human history. As Attlee's government created full employment and the welfare state, ordinary people were given opportunities beyond the dreams of their parents and grandparents. But what is my generation of politicians leaving our children and grandchildren? Britain is the fifth richest nation on earth. We have the power to create a better Britain and contribute to a better world as long as we have the confidence to do so. People are desperate for a new agenda. Now could be the turning point they seek.

CHAPTER FIVE

Ken: A Personal Portrait

Interviewed by
Angharad Penrhyn Jones

Could you give me a flavour of the post-war years, when you were growing up?

I was born just after the European War had ended. In retrospect – though I didn't think it at the time – I grew up in a rather grey and harsh Britain. There was heavy rationing in the first five years of my life and there was still rationing on sweets until I was about 10. If you look at pictures of people from the 1950s, they're all thin. No one was overweight. But we all thought we were doing very well and that things were always getting better. The Labour government created the welfare state and got everyone back into work, and they did it on a fairly equal agenda, so there wasn't any obscene extravagance of the elite as we're seeing now.

And my generation had more than my parents had had. I mean, they'd had fairly grim childhoods. My father's father walked away when he was 14 and he never saw him again. This was after his mother died. He then went off to join the Merchant Navy. My mum's father was killed in the First World War and she became a dancer. Her mum was mentally disturbed and tried to keep her son and daughter completely isolated. So if they ever brought girlfriends or boyfriends home, she'd do everything possible to drive them away. But my parents met in 1940 and fell instantly in love and were just completely besotted with each other. They got married on their third or fourth meeting (*laughs*). And then they just stayed together.

The way they met was quite romantic, wasn't it? Your father was on shore leave and he and two of his shipmates went to a music hall in Workington where your mother was performing.

Yes, he and his friends had had a bit to drink and gone to the music hall and she was dancing on stage. Afterwards they waited by the stage and asked her and the other dancers out for a bite to eat. This was during the blackout and the only place to eat was a fish and chip shop. Then they were on the bus going out to their digs and my father starting singing to my mum, which she found excruciatingly embarrassing (*laughs*). He sang 'I have eyes to see with, but they see only you.' The thing is, they'd never particularly wanted children – I was an accident and so was my sister. They were just completely caught up in each other. And they always were, right up until the day my father died – about 31 years after they met.

Children of parents who are deeply in love can sometimes feel a bit excluded or shut out.

Hmm … Yes, I think we were a bit, though we didn't particularly realise it at the time.

Even though your grandmother refused to welcome your dad into your mother's life, she did live with you for a long time, didn't she?

After they got married my dad moved in with my mum and grandma, but he couldn't stand it so he went back to being a sailor. A few years later, when we lived in a council house, my gran had a minor stroke and moved in with us for around five years until my parents had had enough. My grandmother was this disruptive, nightmare figure, always unpleasant to my father. So they said, we can't take any more of this, you just have to move out. My uncle was living with us at the time as well, so when he moved out to live with his then partner, gran went with him.

Is it true that you didn't socialise with any other kids until you were five, apart from your sister?

Well, we lived in a house above a shop, and there were no other kids around, and there was nothing like nursery school then. Did we visit anyone else? … I don't think so. I don't think I met any other kids until I started school. But my gran was with me all day while my mum was out at work. She could only hobble about on a stick so we'd stay indoors all day.

That sounds quite claustrophobic.

It really was. We didn't have a garden or anything.

Your grandmother used to bully your father to such an extent that you and your mother would be reduced to tears.

She was just rude all the time, I mean just completely rude. She did apologise to him on her death bed, literally in the last hours before she died.

Did that mean a lot to him?

I don't know. My dad was never good at talking about things like that (*laughs*). It was a generation that hid its feelings and emotions.

Were you scared of your grandmother?

No, she was devoted to me, though she wasn't very nice to my sister. I got gastroenteritis when I was a kid, which killed lots of people, there was a huge wave of it in the country. The doctors said I wouldn't live, but my grandmother nursed me through it. My earliest memories are of being propped up on these cushions in the kitchen while she fed me fluids. But it did mean that physically I was around two years behind everyone else. It really retarded my physical development. I didn't catch up until my mid teens.

That must have been hard.

Yes, I mean, when I started my secondary school, with 2,100 boys, I think I was the smallest. And all the sporty things I was hopeless at. I didn't have the strength in my arms to climb up the ropes or jump over the vault. So I grew up with no interest in sports whatsoever. I was a nerdy little boy. I was interested in astronomy because of a radio series called *Journey Into Space*, and then in secondary school I had a very good biology teacher and got caught up in collecting newts in the local park. I became closer to dad when we spent several Sunday mornings together building my first pond.

Did your father talk about fighting in the Second World War?

We knew he'd been sunk but he didn't like to talk about it. He'd spent a couple of days floating around on a boat in the Arctic Sea and had been lucky to survive. He never talked about anything that had happened in his life before he met my mother. It was only after my dad died that his sister would chat about how grim his childhood had been.

He died young, didn't he?

He was only 56. I was 26. Because he'd been a window cleaner, he always looked very healthy, but he'd had a lifetime of always adding sugar and salt and fat to everything. That post-war generation – after the rationing they went mad, eating everything they could get their hands on, and very unhealthy stuff.

He smoked, too.

Yes, he smoked all his life. I remember, just before Tony Blair was elected, big corporations were looking about to see who would represent their interests under a Labour government, and a tobacco industry organisation approached me and said they'd like me to represent them in Parliament. I said no (*laughs*).

Didn't I read that you said, 'You killed my father?'

I think that's what I put in the letter, yes (*laughs*).

I also read that you like Mad Men, *which examines the cynicism of the tobacco industry.*

Oh yes, that's an absolutely wonderful series.

It's very much about women's place in society, too, and I'm interested in your ideas about feminism and your engagement with women's issues – you were ahead of your time.

Well, that's probably because my father and mother were equal. In that post-war period women were in the home and the father owned the house – it was still pretty backward. But my father always treated my mother as an equal – they shared everything, every decision, and my mother always worked. I didn't realise this was unusual at the time.

And your parents treated you and your sister as equals too.

Oh, yes. They never assumed I would do better than her.

Regarding women's rights, I was thinking about your grandmother, who'd had a child – your mother – out of wedlock and then changed the dates on her wedding certificate.

Well, that was a great sin in those days. She'd walked away from her family in her teens because she came home late one night and her father beat her up. She never made any contact with them again. She then got pregnant by a guy she was having an affair with. But he only married her when she'd given birth – clearly he was working on the assumption that if my mother had been born dead, he wasn't going to get married. And you can actually see it on the wedding certificate, all scratched out.

Do you think this experience was in any way at the root of her viciousness?

No, I just think she was profoundly disturbed and it had nothing to do with that. I mean she grew up in a pretty dysfunctional family.

And your Uncle Ken was an interesting character, the man you were named after.

Yes, he was the secretary of the Streatham branch of Oswald Mosely's party. He was the first person in our family not to vote Conservative, and he was voting Fascist (*laughs*). What was bizarre about this was that his entire work was selling cloth to overwhelmingly Jewish tailors all over the East End of London. And when he died in 1986 we discovered that he had a membership card for the National Front. He was virulently homophobic and racist. When the *Radio Times* and *TV Times* came he'd get a big black magic marker and blot out any programme that included homosexuals, blacks, or David Frost (*laughs*). David Frost was dead chuffed when I told him this. I never knew why he loathed Frost. I imagine it was because he was on *That Was The Week That Was*, which was seen as helping to undermine the Tory government. Anyway, Uncle Ken was pretty devoted to me because the three women he married never had any children, and so he was always bringing me toys.

How did he respond to your rise within the Labour movement?

When I became the leader of the GLC, he didn't speak to me for the entire five years I was there. He couldn't believe the things I was saying and doing. I offended everything he believed in. And it was only after the GLC had been abolished that he told my mum he'd like to get together for a meal. We went to the restaurant where Charles de Gaulle used to hold cabinet meetings during the war, and my mum had said we wouldn't discuss anything to do with politics or religion. So we had this final meal where we talked about the Second World War. And then three days later he died. A massive heart attack. You see, he'd been in Burma and had a really grim time. They were always hungry and thirsty. When he came back he committed himself to eating and drinking and became enormous.

Your parents were Tory Party members but they were not homophobic or racist, were they?

This is the thing. My mum had worked with gays and lesbians on the stage. My dad had worked with people of all different races – he worked as a merchant sailor all over the world. So there was no racism or homophobia in our home. Dad was brilliant on race and mum was brilliant on sexuality. So I got the right instincts from each of them.

But you argued with your father about politics.

This is what was so sad about him dying so young. I'd had all these conflicts and tensions with dad, and arguments about everything, and just as I got elected to the council and he was really proud I'd achieved this – then he died. Whereas my mum got to share another 26 years with me. He missed out on all that.

I was really moved by the letter you published in your auto-biography, the letter he wrote to you on your first birthday. He was out at sea and he wrote to you. It's a beautiful letter.

Yes. He was a really wonderful man, actually. Very gentle (*starts crying*).

When you went on the barge with the Queen – you were opening the Thames barrier and your mother went with you – you turned to your mum and said, I wish dad was here.

Yes. He would have loved all of that (*wipes eyes*).

If we could talk about your schooldays for a moment – you just weren't that committed to school, were you? Why was that?

Well, there were 45 kids in my class, and those kids who were well motivated would sit at the front. I tended to sit at the back with my mates and we'd laugh and joke. So I failed my 11 plus. I did a bit better in secondary school but I hated homework and hardly ever did any of it, sometimes cobbled it together in the morning.

Were you easily distracted, bored, or did you hate the rules and regulations?

It was just so boring. I mean, the whole class would just sit there and chant our multiplication tables for hours.

(Laughs) So there wasn't much room for creativity.

Well, the one time I won a prize was for painting. And the O Levels I got were in English Language, English Literature, Art and Geography. The trouble was, there wasn't a culture of this kind of thing at home. My grandmother used to say, you shouldn't have to do homework, it's awful. And no one in my family had ever been to university or even thought about it.

Were there books at home?

No, not many. I started to buy some James Bond books when I did my paper-round and my father would borrow them and read them. And I would get books on astronomy and natural history. But no, we got the television and then watched it for the rest of our lives.

Do you have any regrets about that, looking back?

Oh yes. If I'd grown up in a different environment, undoubtedly I could have got to university. But nobody did. Everybody got a job when they left school, and within a few years they'd earn enough to keep a family. It isn't like that now, when kids go off to get a degree and still can't find any bloody work.

So what did you do when you left school?

I applied for a job at London Zoo and the Gerald Durrell Zoo – I'd read all his books – but they didn't have any vacancies. So I got a job as a technician at a cancer research institute in Fulham Road and spent four years there, and then hitchhiked for five months or so round Africa, then came back and did another four years at a new branch they'd opened in Sutton. The first branch was focused on lung cancer and the second on childhood leukaemia. So during those formative eight years my pattern of thinking and behaviour was set by brilliant scientists. It was all about pursuit of the truth and facts, which doesn't chime well with the world of politics (*laughs*).

They taught you about the importance of empirical evidence?

Yes, and that's always been my approach. I study lots of data before I decide what the policy is. That's why congestion charging worked – we did vast amounts of work. I'm really boring and nerdy like that. In the end, everything is always about detail.

Just to go back a little … I'm interested in the fact that you went hitchhiking in Africa, which was quite an unusual thing to do at the time. Why did you do this?

When I started work at the laboratory I was 17. And on the bus on the way to work I calculated exactly how many times I was going to make that journey before I retired at 65. Because basically, if you got a job with a pension – and no one in my family had ever had a job with a pension before – you didn't move around. This was in 1962. But by 1966 I decided that I didn't want to spend my life safely accumulating a pension. So I went off hitchhiking for five months with my best friend, Mick Towns. Of course, this was the '60s and the whole world was changing.

How did that experience influence you, politically?

Well, it really expanded my horizons, the way that national service or going to university must influence other people. In the middle of the Sahara Desert I met people from the American Peace Corp who wanted to avoid the draft in Vietnam. We had these really good debates about the Vietnam War. But my interest in politics began on the night Kennedy was assassinated. I started reading about American politics. I stayed up all night watching the '64 election. But it didn't occur to me to join anything until 1969. Even in 1968 I was still breeding albino frogs rather than going on marches.

What triggered your decision to join the Labour Party?

When Harold Wilson got elected in '64 I didn't think there was any point joining the party, I thought the government would sort out all our problems. But Wilson disappointed my generation like Blair disappointed the current one. I suppose the exact trigger was when Ollie Olson, who I'd met in Africa, came to Britain to avoid the draft. I joined the Labour Party and got my local MP to help him get a visa. Me and my MP, who was very open, were debating what he should do. And I just fell in love with it all. Suddenly you felt you had real relevance. I went from being a minor figure in the cancer unit to debating what the government and the local council should do.

Isn't this partly why people don't get involved in politics? They feel impotent…

Blair shut the party down. Every year the party branches would debate what motion they were going to send to the Labour Party conference. I used to look forward to going to the conference all year. Day after day you'd have real debate and proper votes. And Blair just turned it into photo opportunities and press conferences and he killed the party, almost. But yes, I just fell in love with it.

Politics has so much to do with timing, and you joined the Labour Party just as everyone else was deserting it because of this sense of disillusionment with Wilson.

I remember my first meeting, almost everyone there was an old-age pensioner. And they said, oh look at our new member. So young! (*Laughs*)

I'm going to read out something you said about this: 'My arrival at the Norwood Labour meeting had been rather like taking a bottle of gin into a room full of alcoholics. I was immediately passed round and consumed.'[1] *So they kind of fell in love with you as well.*

(*Laughs*) I was lucky, there was a good Labour agent who was left-wing and open. If I'd tried to join Islington North Labour Party I wouldn't have been able to. They used to kick everyone out, until Jeremy Corbyn took over.

A lot of people your age were at that time joining far-left parties like the Internationalist Socialists and the Socialist Labour League. They were angry about Vietnam, NHS cuts, attacks on trade unions. So I find it interesting that you were doing the opposite. You described it as being 'like a rat climbing on board a sinking ship'.

If you wanted to achieve something, you needed to join a party that was going to be in government. I had loads of friends in far-left groups, went on lots of marches and all of that. But I wanted to *do* things, not just protest.

You've always said that if you want to change things you've got to do it within the system. You've talked about Gramsci's idea of the long march through the institutions. But what about the role of activists? People who are free to challenge power structures?

That's important too, because that pressure from outside gives those of us who are on the inside the chance to push something through. If the bureaucracy sees there's real pressure building up out there, they try and defuse it, and that means you have to make some concessions. So there can be that relationship between the activists on the street and people like me inside the machine.

In terms of finding your feet inside the machine, it all happened very quickly for you. By the time you went to your second branch meeting you were chairman and secretary of the Young Socialists and on the local government committee. By the third meeting you were membership secretary and on the executive committee. And two years later you were elected a councillor.

Yes. I thought I'd spend the rest of my life in local government. I was only 26 and two years later I was the second youngest member of the GLC. And here we were deciding to scrap motorway schemes, build more housing…

And you'd only just left home yourself. Tell me about your first wife. You were late having romantic relationships and your mother used to worry that you were more interested in reptiles than in girls. But you met Christine at teacher training college.

She was president of the students' union when I was secretary. We got together, but ten years later we split up. I was becoming more and more focused on work and she was about to become a head teacher. I was out most evenings and she came home needing comfort and support, so after a lot of agonising we decided to separate.

So by the time you were 35, you were separated and living alone in a bedsit with your collection of salamanders, and you were in charge of County Hall. Were you at all intimidated or daunted by this?

No, because I didn't anticipate what was going to happen in terms of the media. I just assumed it was going to be really great. I'd been in local government for ten years, I'd been vice-chair of housing in Lambeth and chair of housing in Camden, I'd been a full-time player in all this and I knew what I wanted to do. We'd worked out a really detailed manifesto. What none of us anticipated was that we were going to be demonised as a threat to the West. We were almost depicted as if I were a Soviet agent. If the Tories had decided to ignore me, I would just have had a career in local government. But I turned into this threat to the British way of life.

They did you a favour, then, in a way?

(*Laughs*) But it was rather painful getting there. My poll ratings went down to 18 per cent after three months. Slowly they clawed back. I realised it was a complete waste of time doing newspaper interviews because they just lied. We focused on trying to get on national radio and television programmes, so people can hear you and make up their own minds. There's no way you can get through to the *Mail* and the *Telegraph* reader.

And is this what you'd advise Corbyn to do?

Oh, yes, yes, absolutely.

When you were at the GLC you did away with some of the pomp and ceremony.

I just didn't find any of that terribly interesting. I had to do so much of that ceremonial stuff when I was mayor, and it was a real pain. But the uproar when I didn't go to the Royal

5.1   Ken campaigning against rises in fares for using public transport, 8 March 1982. Photo: G.M. Cookson.

Wedding ... It wasn't just that I'm a republican – I also had no desire to go.

(Laughs) So you hate weddings in general, or... ?

Well, can you imagine what that one would be like? When I got this invitation from the palace my heart sank. And also you were briefed that you should wear an incontinence pad, because you had to get there an hour before it started and it'd be very long and you wouldn't be allowed to move. I mean the idea that I was going to go to the Royal Wedding wearing an incontinence pad had no attraction.

(Laughs) Is that true?

I think it was the head of the ceremonial department who told me this, he said it would be very long.

Suddenly it makes the whole thing seem a lot less glamorous.

(Laughs) I had no desire to be particularly rude to the Royal Family. I actually came to have a lot of respect for the Queen, because she said she'd like to come and open the Thames Barrier, and as Thatcher was abolishing the GLC at the time – well, it was really annoying to Thatcher.

What did you think about Corbyn refusing to sing the national anthem recently?

I thought it was a mistake, because it's been the banner headline of all the gutter press, and it's just not worth it. In retrospect, if I'd known what was coming with the media I'd have been much more cautious about many of the things I said in those first few months. It was only after about two months that the Labour

Party gave us one of their press officers to try to handle this wave of attention. There was no [Peter] Mandelson figure there, or anything like that. There wasn't media training in politics in those days, and all that crap. But there's no shortcut, you only learn through experience, I'm afraid.

Is there any particular thing that stands out for you, something you regret saying or doing?

Well, you can float all these radical ideas, but you need to do it after you've demonstrated that you've done things for people. So you couldn't avoid the issue of Ireland, because we were getting horrific bombings twice a year. But I might have put off launching the lesbian and gay rights policy until we'd cut the [transport] fares. Because that's the biggest single impact the GLC or the mayoralty can have on people's lives.

So how did you deal with being savaged by the media? You were quite young: how did you cope with seeing yourself misrepresented, accused of being unpatriotic, an apologist for murderers – all these terrible accusations?

Well, I was lucky, I had a very supportive relationship with my partner, Kate.

So of all the smear campaigns you've faced, and there are so many of them (both laugh) – you're anti-Semitic, corrupt…

Alcoholic, violent…

Of all of them, which one hurts the most?

(*Sighs*) Hurt would be the wrong word. I could be angry about things that were written. But you know you're dealing with vile people, so it doesn't come as a surprise.

But you must have thought that some people you respect or you know might believe what they were reading?

Well, that's part of the problem. People say, there must be some truth in this story even if it's not all true. But no, they can just make stuff up completely. I'm trying to think – was I ever hurt? Often Kate and I just laughed at this stuff, it was so wildly over the top. A lot of my staff were more outraged by it than I was. But this is what Jeremy's going to go through. This is what the establishment will try to do. If they fear you're going to get in, they'll do anything to try to stop you.

Do you think Jeremy's tough enough to deal with it?

Yes. It's a lot easier coping with this when you're 66 than when you're 35 (*chuckles*).

Did you ever tell yourself that you must have been doing something right if you were getting this kind of response?

Oh yes. I mean once or twice every day someone stops me on the street and says, thanks for all you did, and it's always ordinary people. And so there's a huge chunk of people out there – unfortunately not a majority, otherwise I would have won the last election – who do realise that I'm on their side. That's very sustaining.

And is that partly why, when you became mayor, you didn't choose to live in a plush apartment in City Hall? You stayed in this terraced house. Is it about having your people around you to remind you?

I spent 26 years getting that garden right, and this house is big enough. Look at Jeremy, he lives in just an average house.

Let's talk about you becoming an MP for Brent East. You were there for 14 years. How did you fit into the culture at Westminster?

It's an awful place. I used to hate sitting in the House of Commons with everyone screaming and shouting. I wanted to hear the debate, ask a question, not all this yah booing crap. No, I never liked it at all. Those of us who lived in London and had partners to go back to in the evening would do that, whereas those Labour MPs who were hundreds of miles from home, and lived in some single bedroom flat, would just hang around the bars until the small hours of the morning. So many of the alliances that happened were based on who you were drinking with, rather than politics. I think it's awful if you're an MP for somewhere like Newcastle and you're separated from your family all week. It's a grim life. And that's why so many people drank too much.

So alcoholism was rife?

It wasn't as bad as it was in the '50s and '60s. Then you had about 10 or 12 by-elections a year, because so many MPs dropped dead. It's a bit better now.

I'm wondering – did you ever keep a political diary?

No, there was never time. When I came home from the House of Commons I wanted to cuddle up with my partner, and have a drink. I didn't want to write a sodding diary.

Your mother worked in the music halls. Are you a bit of a showman at heart?

I've never felt that way. I think I'm quite shy. I was quite painfully shy as a kid.

But you wouldn't be presenting chat shows with Janet Street Porter and doing live radio if you were shy, would you?

They're a chance to get your views across. I love doing my Saturday morning LBC radio programme with David Mellor because it's just all about politics. I've ended up doing other things which aren't political, media stuff. And I have to say I'm not greatly enthused by it. It's just a way of reaching out to people.

But I've read that when you were a kid your teachers said you were quite the performer in class.

I can't remember. I droned on to people about astronomy, natural history, things I was interested in. But I just don't remember.

I also read that [KL's deputy] Illtyd Harrington said he had lunch with you and your mother and [actor] Kenneth Williams, and he noticed that you were really performing for your mother. Harrington told your biographer, Andrew Hosken, 'I noticed there was something in Ken's relationship with his mother that he had to be performing and demonstrating'[2] (KL laughs). And you have taken part in performative things, like when you sang with the pop group, Blur.

Well, it was all quite funny, the idea that a mega pop group wanted to do a song with me in it.

Why did they want you?

They asked the prime minister, John Major. They wanted someone with a boring nasal voice. Major wouldn't do it, and I was their second choice.

(Laughs) You didn't take offence?

No, no. I know I've got an awful voice. If I'd had a better voice I might have been prime minister, I don't know. There must be something wrong with my nasal structure – it's so grating, isn't it? *(APJ laughs)* When I was at school I was told, don't sing in assembly, you'll disrupt everyone around you.

You weren't going to go into the music hall then.

Not with my voice.

Well, I think you're a bundle of contradictions and that's one of them. You say you're shy and reserved and I definitely pick up on that. But you are a performer and somebody said you're a great actor and you do spend a lot of time on the stage.

I can't act. I can only be me. I can get up and do my speeches, that's really easy. But if I'm asked to...

How can that be easy if you're shy? Public speaking is one of people's biggest fears.

But I don't find it a problem at all.

So you're shy and not shy? Ok.

We're all contradictions.

Definitely. Somebody said you were the first media politico celebrity and Boris became even bigger. Is that fair? Is that how you'd see it?

I remember when Boris started running for mayor, everyone said it's exactly how it was with Ken, it's all about celebrity. But it wasn't about celebrity with me. The media turn you into that. I was only ever into fares policy and the congestion charge – you know, issues. I don't really care about what my public image is as long as I can get on and do some work. I didn't go into politics to be loved.

So tell me about your relationship with Tony Blair. You worked very closely with him on the Olympics.

Basically, once the congestion charge worked, the relationship changed. I had applied to rejoin the Labour Party in July 2002 and Blair used his control of the NEC to block me. But then six months later the congestion charge comes in and it works, and my poll ratings soar. In July 2003 he sent Sally Morgan, one of his key aides, over to ask if I'd come back and be the Labour candidate. And I said yes. Because I knew, if he was bringing me back to be the Labour candidate, it had to work. We'd get a lot more money. And not just for the Olympics, but key investments, money for extra police, and so on. We had a good working relationship – we just didn't talk about the war, or the issues we didn't agree on. He wanted London to work and I'd still go on my demonstrations against the war and he didn't mind about that.

Are you just very good at compartmentalising, so you can think, well, this is a man who has threatened to destroy me but I want to work with him. Because Blair did threaten to destroy you, didn't he?

Oh yes. And he failed. But then he wants to work with me, so you work with him and get stuff out of him.

Right, so you just don't get bogged down in the emotional stuff.

No, not at all. My wife, if she was here, would tell you she thinks I'm very cold (*laughs*).

Well, I'm really interested in this. So your wife says you are very cold and I think it was Hugo Young who said you're extraordinarily detached. There's this sense that you're quite ruthless, you compartmentalise, have a one-track mind, and you're extraordinarily effective – you've been called the only truly successful socialist of modern times...

Well, it helps if you're not madly hysterical.

Yeah. But at the same time, you clearly have strong emotions about things.

Yes, you can see me weeping occasionally.

There are many references in your autobiography to you crying, actually. You cried during the ceremony for the first civil partnership that you held at the GLC, and this is clearly just an amazing thing that you achieved.

That was so moving. Two lovely old guys who'd been together about 30 years and finally they can come together officially and it was brilliant.

You cried during a speech you gave at City Hall about transatlantic slavery, and also during that incredible speech you gave in Singapore after the 7/7 bombings. You broke down.

I can't think back to that time without being moved to tears because of the pain of it and the number of people that were killed. I can't talk about my father without being close to tears, because we missed … we should have had another 30 years together. I'm not completely inhuman, you know (*laughs*).

But when I think of a lot of political figures, I've never seen them in tears, and you clearly do feel things very deeply.

(*Starts crying*) I feel deeply about a lot of things. But I was brought up in a world where our parents said, don't be loud, it's a bit American. That was that post-war world, we all thought Americans were a bit mad, all this shouting and screaming. So it's a combination – you can have deep feelings, but you don't have to be hysterical all the time.

So how did you cope in Singapore? You were there for the Olympics bid and then the London bombings happened. You're crying now thinking about it. You gave an amazing speech: how did you hold it together?

I barely did. If you watch that speech, at the end my voice is beginning to crack up. I so wanted to be back in London. It was awful. I regret all the time that after we'd won the bid, I stayed on for the victory party. If I'd got the last flight back, I'd have been in London in time.

So that's an eternal regret.

Yes, but in the end, it didn't make any difference, because we'd planned for it all in such detail. We'd known there was going to be a bombing at some point. We'd put all the structures in place. One of the exercises we did was how to respond if both the Commissioner of Police and me had been killed in the initial wave of bombings. We'd closed off a great chunk of central London and simulated a gas attack, things like that.

The speech you gave was celebrated by everyone, regardless of their politics. And you delivered it really calmly. You would have prepared the speech, presumably.

There would be times when I'd be sitting on the Tube, and I'd start to think, what do I say when the bombings come? But I never wrote anything down. Only John Ross asked, what are you going to say when it happens? And I said, I can't talk about it. It wasn't possible. Just before I went off to Singapore, the head of MI5 came to see me and I said, perhaps we've got away with it. She said, no, it's very dangerous out there. So we were waiting for it to happen.

When you found out, you were out shopping for presents for your children. Between then and when you gave that speech, did you call anyone to talk to about the more emotional aspect of it?

When I got back to the hotel it was just lots of phone calls to the police and Transport for London and my staff in London. I swam for half an hour and decided what I was going to say. I couldn't make my speech until Blair had made his, because it would have been a disaster if anything I had to say contradicted what he said. So I waited to see what he said, then went down to deliver my speech.

What was it like when you came back to London? I'm assuming you must have met up with a number of people who'd lost family members or friends.

We had this rally in Trafalgar Square, and all the relatives were there. But I couldn't go to the reception, couldn't cope with it.

I'd talked to the relatives beforehand but I didn't really feel I could sit around with a glass of wine, chatting, all of that (*starts crying*). Also, when I got back it was a question of visiting the sites and the hospitals. One of my staff had had her leg blown off. It was just a horrendous week, very stressful.

I imagine it would have been a very difficult period post 7/7 with a lot of nervousness and paranoia, and then the killing of an innocent man, Charles de Menezes [shot on the Underground by Metropolitan Police]. You stood by the Chief Commissioner, Ian Blair. Was that a difficult decision?

No. Because, I mean, the police occasionally make a mistake. But the defining thing about that was Ian Blair was on television immediately afterwards, apologising. We sent the Assistant Commissioner to visit the Menezes family in Brazil to personally apologise. When Mark Duggan was killed [shot by police in Tottenham in 2011], there wasn't a peep out of City Hall, and when his parents marched to Tottenham police station to complain they weren't allowed in. It was appalling.

But an innocent man lost his life, so shouldn't someone have been held to account for that?

Well, there wasn't any one person responsible. Basically, he had been living in the house where one of the bombers had been. The police followed him when he came out, and then he went on to the Tube, so they just assumed he was going to set off a bomb.

Did that cause you sleepless nights?

Yes, it was awful. I don't generally have sleepless nights, but it was just terrible. But this is the problem. If you've got armed police they will occasionally make a mistake. Just not on the scale you get in America where it's hundreds and hundreds. We're quite good here, only a limited number of police have arms and they've all been very heavily trained. Boris wanted to get rid of Ian Blair because he'd been very good at pushing forward an equalities agenda within the police and had made a lot of changes.

The Daily Telegraph *had wanted him gone for a long time too.*

And the *Mail*. When Boris came in, his powers were increased, so that he could get rid of a Commissioner of Police. I'd not had that power. And on the morning that power kicked in, the *Mail* had a front-page story saying one of Ian Blair's friends had been given a contract from the police and that this was clearly corruption. So Boris demanded his resignation. A year later, the man's completely cleared of course. And then Boris goes and appoints the deputy, whose first speech says something about how they were finished with all this equalities nonsense.

Sometimes when you talk about this stuff I think of The Wire, *which I know you're a fan of. I'm talking about the dirty dealings and the fudging of figures, and the...*

There's also *Homicide: Life on the Street* – have you have ever seen that?

No. It's by David Simon, too.

That's brilliant.

We were talking about the series Mad Men *earlier, which is about the advertising industry – and you've been involved in advertising yourself to raise funds. You've advertised Red Leicester cheese, for example, and a paintbrush. So you were prepared to do whatever it took, as long as it wasn't unethical.*

Well, I didn't mind advertising cheese but I wouldn't have advertised cigarettes.

But you also refused to do a faux-romantic coal advert with [former Conservative MP] Edwina Currie.

Well, we both refused. They wanted this coal advert. You remember the one with the cat and the dog cuddling up? They wanted to follow up with one where Edwina and I would cuddle up and the screen would fade to black just as our lips kissed. And we both thought, oh god. I don't know what they would have paid us.

But you drew the line at that.

Yeah, yeah. I had no desire to kiss Edwina Currie.

(Laughs) If we could go back to that time you were mayor and dealing with this very stressful event: I know this might seem a strange question but after 7/7 did you feel a sense that ... I don't know how to phrase this, but did you feel that you were responsible for the city, almost like a paternalistic feeling that these were your people, this was your city. Does that make sense?

Yes, because I'd grown up in it. And like Sadiq Khan [2016 mayoral candidate for Labour] – we get on very well together – he's grown up here, lived on a council estate. It's a wonderful city to be in now. These great world cities are amazing. But I think London works better than Paris. We're better at integrating different cultures.

You have always given the impression that being Mayor of London was a great honour as well as a big responsibility.

Definitely. Which makes it so frustrating about Boris. He's done bugger all with the job. Just used it to promote himself.

It seems to me that he trades off being a personality.

Well, that's the thing, we all assume he's a great right-wing ideologue but actually he just wants to be there. He wants to be prime minister.

You wanted to be prime minister, didn't you?

Oh I'd love to be prime minister, but to *do* things, not to *be* there. I mean the bloody receptions and all that would be a great bore. But Boris would love all that. The celebrities coming to Downing Street…

It's a sort of culture of narcissism and he's very much part of that. It seems that he deflects any criticism, or any question about what he's actually doing, with a witticism.

He's very affable. He's brilliant at quips. But the next mayor's going to have to move very quickly or London's going to start to be unmanageable very soon – he just hasn't done the work. You look at Cameron and some of these other public school boys and it looks like this smarmy charmy thing is one of the main subjects they teach. He can completely charm people while shafting them.

You said that people who don't know Boris love him and that people who know him loathe him.

The woman who worked with him in Brussels for years – her stuff on him is scathing. And she's worked with him for longer than anybody else. He just uses people, and people think, oh, he's lovely to work for, but the moment they're no longer of any use to him, they're just cut out.

Do you think the opposite might be true of you? That the people who loathe you from a distance because of what they've read about you – they get to know you and then they actually like you? That's something I've heard.

Well, there's no way people couldn't find me better than I'm depicted (*both laugh*). Seriously. Short of being a mass murderer, people are bound to think, he's better than I thought.

Well, a lot of people say you're hard to dislike, even if they hate your politics.

(*Laughs*) Jeremy's facing the same sort of thing at the moment. Everyone says, what a nice man. And he is.

But obviously he's got a ruthless side to him or he wouldn't have even made it this far. I mean a side to him that isn't just 'nice'.

He's principled rather than ruthless. Because he's not run anything since he was on Haringey Council, he hasn't had to be ruthless about anything. He's been involved in campaigns for things he believes in, not deciding who to appoint or who to sack.

So time will tell with all that ... Now, your biographer, John Carvel, says this about you: 'He seems not to have been fitted with the restraining bolt that most politicians have installed somewhere between their minds and their mouths.'[3] *If I could give an example, you called the American ambassador a 'chiselling little crook' for refusing to pay the congestion charge. Is it true that you're missing this restraining bolt?*

I'm occasionally ruder than is probably necessary. But when you think of the crap you have to put up with in politics, it'd be amazing if occasionally you weren't a bit over the top.

You've been described by the Sun *as the most odious man in Britain but you've also come second only to the Pope in the BBC's Man of the Year poll. Why do you think you polarise opinion to such an extent?*

If people read certain newspapers all they get is this completely dishonest tissue of lies and you end up thinking, here's this person who hates Britain and wants to destroy it. And yet, people would have heard me being interviewed on the *Today* programme or they'd have seen me on *Question Time*, and so they'd form a better view. I was quite amazed to come second to the Pope.

But you lost your position as mayor and now a lot of the good work you did is unravelling, essentially. That must be gutting.

But that's politics I'm afraid. It ain't fair and it ain't nice. The media is in the hands of a small elite.

It's easy to forget the repercussions of this in terms of our political system.

The simple fact is, basically, all that we're told about politics, almost all of it is untrue. It's why the left has been driven backwards across most of the Western world at any rate, over these last 30 years. With the hostility, the

5.2　Publicity for an ITV programme on the effects of the abolition of the GLC, featuring a debate between Ken and the minister responsible for abolition planning, Patrick Jenkin, 19 October 1984.

dishonesty, of the media, people just don't get chance to see the truth. Unless you're going to be nerdy like me, poring over economic data.

I assume that most people in politics don't do that.

They all leave it to someone else. Blair left it to Brown. That's what's so good about the appointment of [shadow chancellor] John McDonnell, because, like me, he's focused on the economy.

We've talked a lot about the media – so what do we actually do about their immense power and this dissemination of misinformation and lies?

If you look at independent television, they're covered by OFCOM, who can oversee any bias. Well, I think OFCOM should cover the BBC and the newspapers. Jeremy has said we shouldn't allow people to own too many newspapers. I mean, until Murdoch persuaded Thatcher to allow him to take over so many, we never had that concentration. It was still pretty bad, the majority of them were owned by Tories, but it's just that the balance has shifted so badly. Anyway, let's pause and do a reality check here. In many other parts of the world, someone like me gets assassinated.

But Tony Benn was actually threatened with assassination if he ever became a minister, and you were also warned that you might be assassinated. You've had to cope with genuine threats and had minders ... And you chose your house carefully, so that it wasn't an end-of-terrace, to protect yourself.

I suppose I always worked on the assumption, particularly at the height of all the troubles in Ireland, that I could have been a target for loyalist paramilitary groups. But you know, there's nothing you can do about that.

You also say that a doctor once mentioned that you might have quite low adrenaline levels, which seemed plausible to me when I read about what you've had to deal with.

My family doctor said that. I've always got low blood pressure. I'm just a little laid back.

So you clearly have a high tolerance for stress, danger, risk.

I can cope with all that.

When I think about your political career, I wouldn't have coped with all that stress for a week. Shouldn't politics be able to include people like me?

Well, at least the worst we have to put up with here is losing an election, not a bullet in the back of the head. And this is what the world is about. Who controls the world, the resources, the power. And those that have got it, don't want to let go.

I'd like to ask you about your family set-up because, well, you're seen as quite an unconventional figure. You haven't followed the usual trajectory of powerful political figures and your family set-up is also unorthodox, isn't it?

Well, I lived with Kate Allen for 20 years and she was totally focused, worked for the Refugee Council, and now she's head of Amnesty. And we never intended to have a family, we were totally caught up in our politics. And a friend of mine, Philippa – we'd never been involved with each other – had spent ages trying to find a way to have kids without a partner. And I just said, well look, I'm quite happy if you want to have kids. I'd be happy to take them out to the museum and the zoo and things like that. So she's the mother of my two eldest kids.

And the same is true with Jan Woolf. We became good friends while on the Committee to Stop War in the Gulf in 1991. By that stage I'd had my first daughter with Philippa and we were planning for a second child. Jan and her husband had separated and not had children. She'd changed her mind about not having children, so we had a child together too – Liam, my eldest boy. And then when Kate and I split up, I got involved with Emma. Emma had been waiting to have a family for yonks, so we had our two. So I've got these five kids and these three overlapping families. And oddly enough, after Philippa had had her second daughter with me, she met this great guy and they fell madly in love and had another kid. So for years we've had all these overlapping families going on holiday together. It's a nightmare because you've got to find a villa with 12 bedrooms. But yes, it's unusual. It's been quite fun.

What was interesting, though, was that hundreds of people knew about this, but no one ever told the newspapers. Because when I became mayor and Georgia had just started at secondary school, she'd tell the other kids that her dad was mayor and they didn't believe her. And so I'd go and meet her at the school gates. So many people knew. The Labour Party knew I had an older boy and tried to use it against me in the 2000 campaign. That's just so terrible, the worst sort of Tory-type electioneering. Blair really dragged us down to their standard, he really did.

Do you think that as a society we're still too attached to this bourgeois idea of the nuclear family?

Not really. There's always been many, many more single mums than you'd expect, and many more people who've had children out of wedlock, or had children by an affair and not told their husband. Anyway, it was quite interesting, it must be about five or six years ago, a Republican mayor from Florida came to see me. We went out for lunch and at that stage I hadn't yet married Emma, and I was telling him that I had five kids by three women I wasn't married to, and that I was an atheist. And he said, oh my god, I have to be on my knees in church every Sunday with my family or I don't get elected. So I think London and Britain are way ahead of America on all this.

Yes, that's a hopeful thing.

So much of what passed in the '50s was so repressive. For many people of my generation, the first person they had sex with was the person they married. And so I think an awful lot of people confused the pleasure of sex with being in love. Now, fortunately, my older kids have had relationships, they're not going to make that mistake.

Do you think that by having children with women who looked after them most of the time, it sort of freed you up politically? I'm thinking about the fact that you've been the subject of so much abuse from the media, been stalked, had people root through your bins, all that sort of stuff. And then potential assassinations. Having young children makes you vulnerable, doesn't it, because you worry about them, and you don't want them to be caught up in it. So it was easier to compartmentalise your life.

Well, as I say, until I offered to help Philippa, I never had any plan to have kids at all. I thought that given my dysfunctional childhood I might not be a good dad.

How do you feel about that now?

I'm sure I'm a bit too Victorian in my approach to it all still.

Really? Despite being so progressive?

Having grown up in a world where nothing was ever wasted, I just think of the waste now amongst kids, they get all this stuff and then dump it, it drives me up the wall.

So Victorian in that sense, not in the morality sense.

No, no, no. They've all got into relationships quite early. I think it's been good for them.

I heard you say 'I love you' to your daughter on the phone earlier. You were saying before that men of your generation find it hard to talk about their feelings, and your parents I imagine didn't use that sort of language, or might have been more reticent. Do you feel like you've broken the cycle?

Oh yeah. I'm living with a woman who's 21 years younger than me, and so the style is very different.

So what drew you to Emma, then? Since she's the woman you've had your nuclear family with.

I'm not going to talk about that. All the women in my life have loathed the idea of media attention. If it wasn't for the fact that Emma was working at City Hall and people saw that she was pregnant, we would have kept Tom and Mia out of the media as well. When the guy from the BBC said to me, tell us about all these extra children you've got, these secret children – well, they were not a secret. I just wasn't going to drag them around in front of TV cameras.

Did you find it hurtful when it came out in the press that you were going to be a father and many people thought it was for the first time – this with Emma – and people were making incredibly ageist comments about you?

I just ... everything in the papers is vile. What was annoying was that the *Standard* got hold of it quite early on in the pregnancy, and we hadn't told everybody that we were having a kid. But there's nothing you can do about it, I'm afraid.

Do you think Sadiq Khan [Labour's 2016 mayoral candidate] has got a good chance?

Oh yeah, a very good chance. He'll be up against Zac Goldsmith who has a sort of slightly Boris quality. A fabulously rich person who says what he thinks.

Which is dangerous.

He'll be a formidable candidate. But then, Sadiq will do what I did, which is really rebuild the machine, get the vote out.

And he'll benefit from everything that's happening now.

Well, I found when I was on the phone banks that nine out of ten people I spoke to who were voting for Jeremy were voting for Sadiq, or vice versa.

In terms of the emotional impact of your defeat to Boris in 2008, how was it? You say in your book that you felt a huge sense of loss.

I remember in 1979, when I lost the election in Hampstead, feeling really angry that I'd spent three years doing a massive amount of work and it was all blown away by the stupidity of Callaghan. I remember thinking I never wanted to be in a position where some idiot Labour leader causes me to lose an election again. And then I lost in 2008 because Brown completely screwed up and Labour's vote plummeted to just 24 per cent in that year's local elections.

It's interesting that Blair wanted Richard Branson to be the first Mayor of London.

It wasn't just Branson, they went through so many names. But the thing is, Blair had created a mayoral system where the mayor had so little power, it wasn't going to be terribly attractive to someone who was running a multi-billion pound company. And most of what I achieved was about assembling coalitions with groups outside of City Hall. Blair realised that the system was a mistake and they passed legislation in 2007 that increased the powers of the mayor. So Boris has actually had many more powers than I had. But apart from getting rid of the Commissioner of Police, he's not really used them.

I'm intrigued by the fact that you don't have a history of studying political philosophy. Your thinking is more informed by evolutionary history, anthropology, animal behaviour. You have this theory that we've come from kinship groups, that we've evolved to work co-operatively.

You've got hundreds of thousands of years of us living in extended family groups. All that's been broken down now and atomised, and in a sense you want to try to recreate that. One of the problems is that people have to work such long hours, they don't have as much time to spend with their friends and family as they used to. That's awful – the most significant thing. You look at all these incredibly rich people, they're often not very happy, because there's always someone richer. What's worthwhile about life is your relationships with other people. Friendships and partners and kids. That's what's wonderful. Not how much you earn.

And with your unconventional set-up – I suppose it's kind of like a kinship group when you get together.

Yes, it is. Like some stone age group wandering around.

(Laughs) So you see the world through this lens: you're aware that we as humans are living out of balance with our environment; you're passionate about wildlife; you've seen habitat destruction in Africa. So why is it that you're not a member of the Greens? Because the Labour movement's been slow to respond to the environmental crisis.

Yes, painfully slow, but the Greens aren't going to form a government. Labour will, with a bit of luck, and Corbyn will do a lot on all that. So many Labour Party members quit under Blair and joined the Greens. And I'd be completely at home in the Green Party. But the Greens aren't going to take control.

So what did you think of the Labour strategy, the Parliamentary Labour Party strategy, to try to unseat [Green MP] Caroline Lucas?

I thought it was a disgrace. I'd said to Ed Miliband we should leave Caroline Lucas alone. I'd be quite happy to have a deal with the Greens, so that we identify a few seats they can win, we support them in those and they don't stand in all the others where we need their votes.

What is your approach to environmental issues? How should we minimise our carbon emissions and use of natural resources?

We need an overall economic and environmental strategy. The line I take at the meetings I do around the world is about the importance of getting people out of their cars and onto public transport. Retrofitting all our buildings to be energy efficient. Closing down all our coal and gas stations and switching to renewables. Because if you do that, it's going to create tens of millions of jobs globally as well as saving the environment. But I'm very pessimistic. I think we're clearly heading way beyond two degrees [the threshold after which climate change is thought to be especially dangerous]. And I'm really worried about what sort of world it's going to be mid century, and what my kids are going to face. Part of the problem is that scientists always understate things. And politicians in dialogue with climate change scientists just hear what they want to hear.

What worries me is the fact that economic growth is coupled with resource depletion. And that the aviation industry is just going from strength to strength.

We've got to move away from a society based on what you own, to one based on your relationships. The whole economy is just about increasing consumption and it's going to be catastrophic. But oh God, we're so far away from getting that across to people.

Isn't it partly that it's so horrific that we struggle to conceptualise it? Denial sets in…

My worry is that by end of the century you've just got a few hundred thousand people living in the Arctic or something. So much of where we currently live will be uninhabitable. There'll be catastrophic loss of life. But until then, I suspect many of the political and corporate interests aren't going to move.

And we'll be beyond the tipping point by then, if we're not already beyond it. Would you agree with Naomi Klein – the idea that you can't tackle climate change without having a different economic model?

That's it, you've got to move away from encouraging people to buy more things.

But the Westfield shopping mall was part of the Olympics project – that's all based on people consuming, isn't it?

Yes, but they owned a big chunk of the land, and we had a simple choice of integrating their development with the Olympics, and of course, the defining thing about that is that people mainly go there by public transport. That's one of the biggest things to make an impact on climate change: get people out of cars.

I'm also aware that often with these big projects it's the big corporations that tend to profit because they put the money in.

On a project of that scale you're only going to get mega corporations able to do it. It's a vast development.

So you call yourself a loony lefty but you're working with big corporations who are making heaps of money. There is a tension there, isn't there?

No, not really. Look at say, housing. When I became mayor the planning law was that 25 per cent of new homes built should be affordable. I doubled it to 50 per cent. And these big companies knew I was going to insist on 50 per cent, unless they could prove it wasn't financially viable. And what was interesting – the amount of housing being built during my administration *doubled*. And as soon as Boris got in, it halved. So the idea that setting a fair target will discourage business is crap. They did more. And I mean, if you're going to hold office, you've got to deal with large corporations, unpleasant governments, lots of very nasty people, otherwise you shouldn't bother to go into politics.

So let's end on a positive note, because we've talked about some quite depressing things. Let's talk about the pleasures you take from life. The gardening you do.

Yes, I love gardening. I just wish I'd known as much about gardening in the beginning as I do now – I could have avoided some of the errors I made.

But that's like a metaphor for life, isn't it?

Yes, it is, it is.

So what do you do on an average day now?

I get the kids to school, walk the dog, do the shopping, potter in the garden. About ten times a year I go abroad to do a lecture. I was in Brazil last week for the annual conference of mayors and they wanted me to talk about transport policy.

So how has that been for you? Because it's quite a contrast to running a city.

I hate not running things. But I've just done my life the wrong way round. I was 45 when my eldest girl was born. Now I'm 70 and have these five kids. But having been out to meetings so much, it is really nice being at home in the evening with the family. I do like it. Sitting around watching the telly, cooking

5.3 Ken with his dog Coco in his Cricklewood garden, December 2015. Photo: Jan Woolf.

meals. And one of the things that haunts me slightly – I was 26 when my dad died. I know the pain I felt. By the time I'm in my mid 80s, Tom and Mia will be in their mid twenties. I'm not going to be around to their dotage, so I want to spend time with them now.*

* Since this interview was conducted, Ken has been drawn back into the political limelight after being appointed to serve as co-convenor of Labour's Defence Review.

So when the telly's on and Boris is being interviewed, or Blair's coming on to say that Corbyn supporters should get a heart transplant, do you find yourself shouting at the telly and wanting to intervene?

I never shout at the telly. If you've been through all the shit I have, you get used to coping with it all (*laughs*).

CHAPTER SIX

'I Don't Know Much About Art But ... '

by Jan Woolf

... a lot of artists showed a considerable amount of support for Ken Livingstone. I first met him when I was a Haringey art teacher, setting up a show, *Kids for Peace*, at the Institute of Education in 1981. It was CND meets Blue Peter, and I'd invited him to open it as the new leader of the GLC. But the Institute had dis-invited him as too controversial a figure; his press was very undermining. He turned up anyway and asked me to put the work up later in the foyer of County Hall. It was this chutzpah that many artists liked, empathising with the notion of the eccentric (literally meaning outside the circle) politician. But Ken operated inside and outside most circles, dragging the marginalised into the mainstream.

At the time, I'd just turned in my dissertation on Gustav Courbet, the great nineteenth-century painter and Paris Communard, who famously said *I paint no angels for I see no angels*. The two figures were linked in my mind, for Courbet, like Ken, was a materialist, and related to the reality of people's lives rather than the romantic or utopian. Ken also knew that art changed people's consciousness, and it was this, rather than votes, that drove the GLC's Arts and Recreation Committees of the 1980s. Ken was making all sorts of things possible for Londoners, and those committees, chaired by Tony Banks, produced an explosion of art forms from all sectors of London life. This was quite unlike the old Labour paternalism; it was rather art as agency, making London's minorities culturally more visible and giving credibility to that expression. The GLC committees also brought formerly minor arts to the fore, like video, photography, printmaking, pop music and community radio – giving them a fine-art validity; promoting them, if you like, up the ladder of elitist art forms. It can be argued that this fertilised art-making today, as it could borrow from and be influenced by these forms, producing something new in a dialectic of creativity in a major multicultural world city.

The GLC manifesto of 1981 was crawling with art, and Ken was letting people who knew about the arts get on with it. They had the freedom to advise, support and commission, and this harnessed the energy of knowledge and enthusiasm well – even if it was outside Ken's comfort zone. These were non-voting, advisory committees that were fostering Community Art. The emphasis here was on the group and social side of art-making rather than individual achievement – at a time before the relativism of postmodernism was in its full pomp, when art thinking fished in the clearer waters of Stuart Hall's 'cultural studies'.

There was huge support for Black Arts in London from the GLC's Arts and Recreation Committees; *Black* incorporating all immigrant experience as well as feminist, gay and disabled. New art forms were putting taproots into the mainstream – right for what needed to be expressed 'here and now' rather than as traditional ethnic or folk exotica.

All this feels retro now, but as part of Britain's cultural heritage it did form the creative and political background for many of today's successful artists, creating the material conditions in which they could flourish. Nor should the impact of the GLC's Freedom Pass be underestimated. Creativity is often on a slow burn, many 60 plus's getting around the city for free, nipping into galleries, knocking out bits of writing on park benches – meeting others. Older, established artists too, cross-pollinating ideas in the capital, meeting up for a chat and a grumble.

To me, aesthetics means a coherent order of things that excites and satisfies the mind and the emotions, and much human activity has this, not just art. Political campaigning, like art, is a focusing of different kinds and intensity of intelligence. And it's in the spirit of 'you can't have half a mind to struggle' that you do what you choose to do well – no half measures. The energy and headspace required for politics often excludes the arts, and Ken would be the first to admit that he'd not kept up with the labyrinthine nature of artput. But he knew that creativity should be nurtured and supported. OK, they (politicians) all say that, but Ken drew a lot of support from visual artists who donated work for funding his later campaigns to be Mayor of London.

6.1   *Haywain with Cruise Missiles*. Peter Kennard 1980. Photomontage. Tate.

While leader of the GLC he was introduced to Peter Kennard by Hilary Wainwright. Ken had done his research and recognised in Peter the true heir of John Heartfield, the artist most famous for his photomontage exposing Hitler's links with big business, with the cash being placed in the open, backward arched hand of the Führer's 'Sieg Heil'. Peter was already known for his photomontage *Haywain with Cruise Missiles*, and Ken invited him to express in visual terms many of the GLC's policies on peace and economics.

By breaking down elements in photographs, cutting them up and reconstituting them, a critical narrative on opposing futures can be presented visually. (Peter Kennard, *Images for the End of the Century*)

This ability to make an image that presents an idea in the blink of an eye (the psychologists call it a Gestalt) was something Peter did well – and Ken liked that no-bullshit element. His work was well suited to a GLC that needed a strong visual punch as well as aesthetic grace, so Peter became a sort of County Hall artist-in-residence. He was also working with CND in getting his images out on demonstrations and developing a public art. His exhibition at County Hall in 1983, for GLC peace year, was opened by the historian E.P. Thompson, quoting Shelly: *We must imagine what we know.*

During Ken's backbench wilderness years, he and Peter had stayed friendly and Ken was invited to speak from within Peter's installation *Welcome to Britain* (1994) at the Royal Festival Hall, a space once controlled by the GLC. The work was an apparent shipwreck of debris: pallets, placards, images of homelessness. Ken, his face lit by a portable red traffic light, became an integral part of the work as he spoke into a microphone. His presence changed the work – a voice speaking of homelessness nailed the installation to a specific issue. His talk was compelling, like a moving mouth in a Beckett play. The work went on to galleries in Liverpool, Cambridge and Folkestone. Should the bottom really drop out of politics, here was a ready-made career.

6.2   Ken with Peter Kennard at *Welcome to Britain*, Folkestone 1994. Photo: Jenny Matthews.

Then there was the inclusion of Ken as the kinaesthetic art element (i.e. he moved) in Peter's installation *Our Financial Times* at Gimpel Fils – Peter's New Bond Street gallery run by René Gimpel, who offered his gallery twice for fundraising auctions for Ken when he was standing for mayor. This installation required him to walk through a long line of placards, talking about third world debt, the IMF and the

World Bank. He wove through the detritus of protest, speaking his socialist credo, at each twist and turn bringing something else into focus: the destruction of our manufacturing base, the corruption of the right-wing press, international outrages, and so on. At the end he picked up another microphone and walked back again. It was electrifying, the words and images together making their own power, producing new emotion. At the end of the opening performance Ken put the mic down, picked up the last placard and walked out of the gallery with it towards Claridges, a hundred yards away. This was unscripted and powerful, an extraordinary sight, the lone demonstrator walking through the heart of Mayfair with a placard protesting third world debt, people staring at him. Gobsmacked. As if the ex-GLC renegade, the bored backbencher, had taken to the streets. There were six performances but none as powerful as that first one. It made it on to *Have I Got News For You* – as a joke of course, completely missing the seriousness and passion of the event.

Peter and I went on to work together on many art/politics campaigns, several involving Ken. I asked Peter some questions.

JW: Your art is famously politically engaged. Do you think all art is? Even subliminally?

PK: All art is political in that it mirrors the time that it was made. But some work is actually engaged in trying to critique the politics of the society we live in. Like mine.

JW: Now you have a retrospective at the Imperial War Museum. There's a picture of Ken there, in one of your installations. Would you say this is ironic, or an example of what goes around comes around?

6.3   Ken performing in Peter Kennard's *Our Financial Times*,
Gimpel Fils 1995. Photo: Jenny Matthews.

PK: On the opening night of the exhibition, I was
showing some IWM dignitaries round, and we stopped
at a photograph of my *Welcome to Britain* installation, in
which Ken appeared. As I was telling them about my GLC
years with Ken, a distinct voice from behind us said 'Do
you remember when we did this Peter?' The dignitaries
were agog.

JW: Anything to add on this interesting collaboration between artist and politician?

PK: My work at the GLC was the most fertile collaboration I've ever had with an institution, as it allowed my work to be seen by everybody, free of charge, and available outside the art gallery system. It also enabled me to work with someone who respected the independence of the artist, and to use the work in relation to what's going on politically. It was a great time.

Ken's bid for mayor required some arts proclamations, and here he is in *Arts Quarterly*, the National Arts Collection Fund journal (Spring 1999):

Unlike wine, good food and cinema, the visual arts have played a peripheral part in my life. I've BEEN art though … I recently consumed some too – the Turner prize contenders at the Tate. As vice president of London Zoo I related well to Chris Ofili's paintings made of elephant dung, and enjoyed immensely Cathy de Monchaux's work, which reminded me of the *Alien* films. I have a socialist's leaning towards good polemical art, but friends consider me visually semi-literate. Art touches us all however. For artists it's all consuming. For the rest of us it's just there, enriching our lives: and like air or water it should be free. Or as much of it as possible.

The Free for All Museums campaign, which I was integrally involved in through my union BECTU's artists' branch, had won its fight against the plan to impose entry charges for publicly funded collections – with the then Culture Secretary Chris Smith declaring continued free entry in 2000, through a VAT anomaly worked out by the National Arts Collection

Fund. Ken had supported the Free for All campaign, proclaiming in the same article:

> I've never been a promoter of Victorian values, but they did have one or two good ideas. As part of the extension of our public life the Victorians built many of our finest museums. Free entry, as at the British Museum a century earlier, was assumed for the enjoyment and instruction of everyone. During Thatcher's monetarist tyranny, when public subsidy for the arts was withdrawn, the South Ken museums were virtually privatised … I supported the Free for All campaign, calling for the preservation of free entry to all our publicly funded museums … My interest in science was fired up by short and regular visits to the Science Museum as a boy. Later, as a lab technician at the Royal Marsden Hospital, I knew of many cancer patients who dropped into the nearby V&A for sustaining visits during long periods of treatment – less likely at a fiver a time.

Ken knew that increasing public ownership of art would put people in a different psychological relationship with it, whether inside or outside a museum, removing the notion that art is just for the middle or upper classes. It's for everyone, to make of what they will.

The Auctions

I organised three of the *Bid for Ken* art auctions to raise funds for the mayoral campaigns in galleries in Mayfair, Clerkenwell and Islington. They were all great galleries, contenders on the arts scene, representing good artists. Setting these up was a joy – involving conversations not just with the artists, but also gallerists, framers, designers, printers and caterers; the industry of art. Curating, showing, art at the service of politics, yet not dipping at the knee or doffing the cap. 'Art as an expression of personal freedom', as Antony Gormley was quoted at the top of one of the terrific catalogues designed by Jenni Boswell-Jones and Ismail Saray of *AND* magazine in Whitechapel.

2000   The first auction was organised by Gimpel Fils gallery and raised money for Ken's campaign as an independent candidate in the mayoral election. Many art stars had given work – Damian Hirst, Maggi Hambling, Sarah Lucas, Howard Hodgkin and others. Polly Toynbee's rather caustic piece in the *Guardian* about this 'glitterati event' advised us to 'keep these worlds (art and politics) apart or risk cross contamination and mutual foolishness', citing a particularly ripe rant by Tracey Emin. But she'd missed the point, for when these worlds come together you get something quite different. With artists of this profile just giving is in itself political. Yet art and politics have always fused – even if there is an art cult, divorced from ordinary life and people. But when the cult makes a political choice like this, it's interesting. They saw Ken as a rebel, standing against the odds, or in Ken's case the Blairite Labour Party. In her piece, Polly Toynbee also brought up the Free Museums issue, which Ken vocally supported and Blair didn't – with Chris Smith that notable exception within the Labour cabinet. In lamenting Labour's lost opportunity in declaring museums free in the next budget, she said that Ken could carry on 'having fun with the issue'. Having fun? This was deeply serious to us all.

2004   Victoria Miro's Wharf Gallery hosted the auction, with the added value of Anthony Caro, Ralph Steadman, Isaac Julian, Susan Hiller joining the catalogue. Less well-known artists gave too, and showing in this company helped their careers. A photograph by Christopher Stewart, for example, was bought by the curator of photography at the V&A. Ken auctioned the first Lot – a montage *Peace on Earth* by Peter Kennard – as he could talk knowledgably about it, linking the work to the GLC's peace committee.

2008 We get a Banksy for the auction at the Aquarium L-13 on Farringdon Road, a site bombed by Zeppelin L-13 in 1915. They've now moved premises and have become the *L-13 Light Industrial Workshop and Private Ladies and Gentlemen's Club for Art, Leisure and the Disruptive Betterment of Culture* in Clerkenwell – one of the best art spaces in town. Their 'Assistant for Mayor' campaign was a hilarious and visual iconoclastic swipe at the inane rhetoric of election propaganda. Instigated by Steve Lowe, the artist/owner of L-13, the majority of the posters were designed by Steve and Adam, aka the art couple Harry Adams (at point of publication, still together). They thought that 'in the spirit of democracy and fair play' they should oppose Ken as well as support him, and are still very impressed that he went along with it all. They also invited other L-13 artists, like Billy Childish and James Cauty, to contribute. We had a Jeremy Deller photo, even something from Pure Evil, incorporating the edgy Shoreditch crowd with blue-chip Mayfair. Those very fine painters Jo Wonder and Geraldine Swayne gave work, and the Banksy painting (*Sketch for Essex Road* – a paint sketch for a wall art work) mysteriously appeared and was bought at £195,000 by his own gallery. It created a terrific buzz, with live bidding from the USA. Somebody from New Labour turned up to help with a flowchart and a clipboard and got in the way.

2012 It was back to Gimpel Fils as Ken contested the mayoralty of Boris Johnson. The highest profile artist was Anish Kapoor, though his contribution didn't sell on the night. But we had a painting by Bob and Roberta Smith, *Reasons to Vote for Ken*, paintings from Derek Ogbourne and Jill Rock,

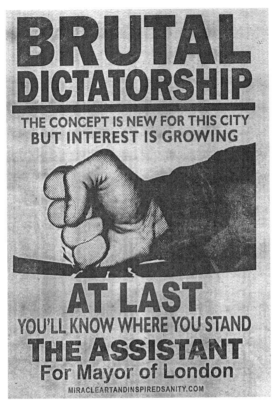

6.4   *Brutal Dictatorship*. The Assistant for Mayor policy
poster 2008. The Assistant, aka Steve Lowe and Adam Wood.
The Assistant produced a series of 'policy posters' for the
Aquarium auction in 2008, reasoning, in the interests of
balance, that they should be as much against him as for him.

and great photography from Roelof Bakker and Charlie
Hopkinson. Then there were two historic James Boswell
lithographs donated by his widow, Ruth Boswell, instigator of
the Naming of the Dead event in Trafalgar Square on the eve of
Bush's re-election. Ken had allowed the Square to be used for
this. Another great art/politics connection in this auction was

Photo-op, by kennardphilipps, an iconic image, in the best and true sense of the word.

These auctions were events in themselves, with many of the artists turning up for a drink and a canapé, and to hear Ken attempting art patter from the front, sparring with the organisers. *I don't know much about art but I know what I like… Is that one the right way up... My mum would have loved that*, and so on, deliberately playing on his slightly philistine image, and then letting the professional and persuasive auctioneer Chris Knapton get on with his job.

With Ken as mayor, London had opened up for political enquiry, and even dissent. In 2003 Trafalgar Square was transformed by the pedestrianisation of the road between the Square and the National Gallery, and the Mayor of London's fourth plinth commission was set up with competitions that brought new contemporary sculpture to the Square. On the eve of the invasion of Iraq, Ken had allowed the Committee to Stop War in the Gulf to use City Hall for *London Says, Not in Our Name* – an event declaring opposition to war completely 'within the aims and objectives of the GLA'. Harold Pinter was there, reading blinding new poetry, and Bridget Riley, who'd also supported the Free Museums Campaign, gave a print for auction. Ralph Steadman, a stalwart of the auctions as well as the anti-war movement, was there too, and made a poster with copies signed by all participants.

Become a Man, a new play by Richard Bradbury about the escaped slave Frederick Douglass, was produced at City Hall for the 200th commemorations of the abolition of slavery in 2007. An exhibition, *Rebels and Trouble Makers*, went up in the foyer, with new photographic portraits by Geoff Woolf of Harold Pinter, Peter Tatchell, Tony Benn, Sivanandan, Doreen Lawrence and Bob Crow, and painted portraits by Jolie Goodman of Walter Wolfgang, Brian Haw, Helen John and Camila Batmanghelidjh, people whose work and activism has now hit the mainstream, to varying degrees. I remember the inveterate peace campaigner Brian Haw, on the opening night, calling up through the spiralling spine of the building to 'Ken the quisling'. Of course, Ken had his enemies, in this instance as a result of the attempted removal of Brian's peace camp at Parliament Square as a health hazard. With Ken, contradictions abound.

The last thing Ken did as mayor was to free up the Leake St tunnel at Waterloo for Banksy's *Cans Festival* of wall art. It opened on the evening of the day Ken lost the mayoralty to

6.5   *Sketch for Essex Road.* Banksy. Sold at Bid for Ken, Aquarium gallery 2008.

Boris Johnson; a group of us were there speculating on the support Johnson might have got from artists! But the next morning, his first without a political role, Ken turned up with his two youngest children, admiring the work on the wall. Not a gallery – a wall. In London.

Jan Woolf is a playwright, arts organiser, and chair of the Left Book Club.

Notes

Preface

1. www.bbc.co.uk/news/uk-politics-22073434

1 The GLC Years

1. Mike Ward chaired the GLC's Industry and Employment Committee and was deputy leader in the GLC's final year.
2. Doreen Massey is now Emeritus Professor of Geography at the Open University.
3. The Greater London Enterprise Board was set up by the GLC as a publicly owned, independently run company which pursued both profit and not-for-profit activities.
4. Patrick Abercrombie, *Greater London Plan*, University of London Press, 1944.
5. Discussed in more detail on p. 135.
6. Ken Livingstone, *You Can't Say That*, Faber & Faber, 2011, p. 255.
7. Livingstone, *You Can't Say That*, p. 253.
8. Andrew Hosken, *Ken: The Ups and Downs of Ken Livingstone*, Arcadia Books, 2008.

2 The GLA Years and Beyond

1. Ken's relationship with his older children is discussed on p. 155.
2. Christian Wolmar, 'Tube PPP reaches end of the line', *Guardian*, 18 December 2009.
3. Duncan Bowie, *Politics, Planning and Homes in a World City*, Routledge, 2010, p. 228.
4. Doreen Massey, *World City*, Polity Press, 2007.
5. See pp. 143–6.

6. Ken Livingstone, *You Can't Say That*, Faber & Faber, 2011, Chapter 16.

7. This interview took place before Ken was appointed to co-chair Labour's Defence Review.

8. Ken Livingstone, *If Voting Changed Anything They'd Abolish It*, Fontana Press, 1988.

3 Boris Will Be the Death of Me

1. Alex Crowley, *Victory in London: The Inside Story of the Boris Campaign*, Bretwalda Books, 2012.

2. www.mirror.co.uk/news/uk-news/tories-several-candidates-next-mayor-3957829

3. www.thejc.com/comment-and-debate/analysis/35741/analysis-her-love-us-sadly-unrequited

4. www.economist.com/node/16994485

5. Crowley, *Victory in London*, p. 57.

6. www.dailymail.co.uk/news/article-2234565/Lynton-Crosby-Foul-mouthed-abuse-campaign-chief-revealed-lands-Tory-post.html

7. Crowley, *Victory in London*, pp. 149–50.

8. Crowley, *Victory in London*, p. 104.

9. Crowley, *Victory in London*, pp. 109–10.

10. Crowley, *Victory in London*, pp. 130–1.

11. Crowley, *Victory in London*, p. 133.

12. Crowley, *Victory in London*, p. 165.

13. Crowley, *Victory in London*, p. 184.

14. Crowley, *Victory in London*, p. 189.

15. Crowley, *Victory in London*, pp. 192–3.

16. 2012/apr/19/lord-sugar-tweets-ken-livingstone

17. Crowley, *Victory in London*, pp. 201–2.

18. www.theguardian.com/politics/2011/oct/21/ken-livingstone-you-cant-say-that-memoir

19. www.theguardian.com/commentisfree/2013/jul/16/cant-nurture-families-and-uproot-them

20. www.telegraph.co.uk/news/uknews/1453173/The-extra ordinary-world-of-Andrew-Gilligan.html
21. www.theguardian.com/politics/2012/feb/29/boris-johnson-london-mayor-elections
22. www.dailymail.co.uk/debate/article-2215342/If-Boris-Johnson-Prime-Minister-Im-plane-Britain-says-Max-Hastings.html
23. www.thesundaytimes.co.uk/sto/newsreview/features/article 777790.ece
24. www.theguardian.com/commentisfree/2012/aug/05/sonia-purnell-boris-johnson-not-prime-minister-material

4 Rebuilding the Party, Rebuilding Britain

1. www.theguardian.com/technology/2013/may/28/obama-chinese-president-cyber-attacks
2. See Chapter 1, pp. 24–5.
3. John Ranelagh, *The Agency: The Rise and Decline of the CIA*, Simon & Schuster, 1987, p. 85.
4. Harold Macmillan (ed. Peter Catterall), *The Macmillan Diaries: The Cabinet Years 1950–1957*, Macmillan, 2004, p. 509.
5. Ken Silverstein and Alexander Cockburn, 'Major U.S. Bank Urges Zapatista Wipe-Out', *Counterpunch*, Vol. 2, No. 3, 1 February 1995.

5 Ken: A Personal Portrait

1. Ken Livingstone, *If Voting Changed Anything They'd Abolish It*, Collins, 1987, p. 11.
2. Andrew Hosken, *Ken: The Ups and Downs of Ken Livingstone*, Arcadia Books, 2008.
3. John Carvel, *Citizen Ken*, Chatto & Windus, 1984, p. 107.

THE RENT TRAP

How We Fell into It,
and How We Get Out of It

by Samir Jeraj and Rosie Walker

'It is time to change what is possible.
Rents are too high.
The quality of what is rented is too low.
Rights are minimal. The market has failed.
Rosie Walker and Samir Jeraj have explored all
the possible escape routes and found the way out.'

Danny Dorling, author of *Inequality and the 1%*
and *All That is Solid*

Available from March 2016 from Pluto Press
and the Left Book Club.

www.plutobooks.com
www.leftbookclub.com

SYRIZA
Inside the Labyrinth

by Kevin Ovenden
with a Foreword by Paul Mason

'A fascinating, humane, caustic analysis of
Greece and the rebirth of its left –
an inspiration for progressives everywhere'

Zoe Williams, the *Guardian*

'Mesmerising ... Ovenden cuts through
stereotypes and ignorance to tell the
story of the Greek resistance'

Paul Mason

Available now from Pluto Press and the Left Book Club.

www.plutobooks.com
www.leftbookclub.com